Writing for a purpose

PHOTOCOPIABLES

impact

WRITING HOMEWORK

Published by Scholastic Ltd,
Villiers House,
Clarendon Avenue,
Leamington Spa,
Warwickshire CV32 5PR

© 1996 Scholastic Ltd
1 2 3 4 5 6 7 8 9 6 7 8 9 0 1 2 3 4 5

UNIVERSITY OF NORTH LONDON

Activities by the IMPACT Project at the University of North London, collated and rewritten by Ruth Merttens, Alan Newland and Susie Webb

Editor Jane Bishop
Assistant editor Sally Gray
Designer Louise Belcher
Series designer Anna Oliwa
Illustrations Brian Hoskin and James Alexander
Cover illustration Hardlines, Charlbury, Oxford

Designed using Aldus Pagemaker
Printed in Great Britain by Clays Ltd, Bungay, Suffolk

British Library Cataloguing-in-Publication Data
A catalogue record for this book is available from the British Library.

ISBN 0-590-53376-2

All rights reserved. This book is sold subject to the condition that it shall not, by way of trade or otherwise, be lent, hired out or otherwise circulated without the publisher's prior consent in any form of binding or cover other than that in which it is published and without a similar condition, including this condition, being imposed upon the subsequent purchaser.

No part of this publication may be reproduced, stored in a retrieval system, or transmitted, in any form or by any means, electronic, mechanical, photocopying, recording or otherwise, without the prior permission of the publisher. This book remains copyright, although permission is granted to copy pages 6 to 10; 13 to 40, 43 to 70, 73 to 98 and 101 to 127 for classroom distribution and use only in the school which has purchased the book, or by the teacher who has purchased this book and in accordance with the CLA licensing agreement. Photocopying permission is given for purchasers only and not for borrowers of books from any lending service.

Thanks to Gail E.Tompkins for ideas included in Writing Cube, page 119 first published in Teaching Writing (Merrill 1994).

Crown copyright is reproduced with the permission of the Controller of HMSO.

KEY STAGE TWO CONTENTS

IMPACT WRITING HOMEWORK

Introduction	5–6
Parents' letter	6
Parents' booklet	7–10

Year 3

Teachers' notes	11–12
Table organiser	13
The rules of the game	14
What's outside?	15
The special award	16
Stranded!	17
Hostage teddy	18
Game instructions	19
'Cockles and mussels, alive, alive oh!'	20
'How to open'	21
Knock, knock…	22
New Year resolutions	23
Chocolate heaven!	24
The best and worst of TV	25
Diwali	26
Sweet tooth	27
Angry!	28
These are a few of my favourite things	29
Where do I go?	30
Best foot forward!	31
Sandwich maker	32
Happy birthday to you!	33
Oi! Tidy up your bedroom!	34
Seal of approval	35
We're talking telephone numbers!	36
Nearly new!	37
Talking pages	38
In *my* day!	39
Open to persuasion	40

Year 4

Teachers' notes	41–42
Post it!	43
'Doctor, doctor…'	44
Local hero	45
Neighbours	46
Babysitter	47
Mugshots	48
'An apple a day…'	49
Postcard message	50
Exciting foods	51
Many happy returns	52
Merry Christmas!	53
This is your life!	54
Musical words	55
The sound of music	56
Model instructions	57
Just my cup of tea	58
Looking for work!	59
School signs	60
Road safety campaign	61
Message in a bottle	62
Magic beans	63
This is how you write a letter…	64
Media slogan	65
Front page news	66
Atlas of my world	67

KEY STAGE TWO
CONTENTS

Please Miss!	68
Send out for pizza!	69
The image of music	70

Year 5

Teachers' notes	71–72
Weather forecasting	73
Playground rhymes	74
Pen-friend	75
This is me	76
Captions	77
Breakfast instructions	78
It makes me so angry!	79
It's just not good enough!	80
'I say, I say, I say…'	81
Healthy lunchbox	82
Sweet or savoury?	83
Can you cook?	84
Remember! Remember!	85
Spend! Spend! Spend!	86
Carnivore or herbivore?	87
This is your life!	88
Pros and cons	89
Keep it simple!	90
Save the whale	91
Believe it or not	92
I can icon	93
Thank you for nothing!	94
Watch this space	95
Step by step	96
Cause and effect	97
Address book	98

Year 6

Teachers' notes	99–100
TV survey	101
Personal advertisement	102
Wanted!	103
Stop the press!	104
Saga in fifty words	105
Calling Iceland	106
Phone book	107
Magazine freebies	108
Note-taker	109
Long time no see	110
Improving your environment!	111
Home rules	112
There should be a law against it!	113
Legalise it!	114
Sporty points	115
Agony Aunt or Agony Uncle?	116
Family album	117
Lonely hearts	118
Writing cube	119
Mad menu	120
Memory tags	121
What a giveaway!	122
Vicious circles	123
It's a fact!	124
Read all about me!	125
TV teacher	126
With deepest sympathy	127
Afterword	128

impact
WRITING HOMEWORK

impact
INTRODUCTION

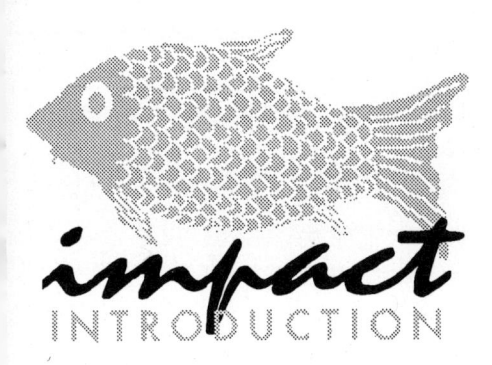

IMPACT books are designed to help teachers involve parents in children's learning to write. Through the use of interesting and specially developed writing tasks, parents can encourage and support their child's efforts as they become confident and competent writers.

The shared writing programme is modelled on the same process as the IMPACT shared maths which encompasses a non-traditional approach to homework.

This is outlined in the following diagram:

> The teacher selects a task based on the work she is doing in class. The activity may relate to the children's work in a particular topic, to the type of writing they are engaged in or to their reading.

⇩

> The teacher prepares the children for what they have to do at home. This may involve reading a particular story, playing a game or having a discussion with the children about the task.

⇩

> The children take home the activity, and share it with someone at home. This may be an older brother/sister, a parent or grandparent or any other friend or relation.

⇩

> The parents and children respond to the activity by commenting in an accompanying diary or notebook.
> * This mechanism provides the teacher with valuable feedback.

⇩

> The teacher uses what was done at home as the basis for follow-up work in class. This may involve further writing, drawing, reading or discussion.

The activities in this book have been designed to enable children to develop and expand their writing skills in conversation with those at home. Where possible the activities reflect the context of the home rather than the school, and draw upon experiences and events from out-of-school situations.

Shared activities – or homework with chatter!

Importantly, the activities are designed to be shared. Unlike traditional homework, where the child is expected to 'do it alone' and not to have help, with IMPACT they are encouraged – even required – to find someone to talk to and share the activity with. With each task we say the following should be true:
- something is said;
- something is written;
- something is read.

Sometimes the main point of the IMPACT activity is the discussion – and so we do try to encourage parents to see that the task involves a lot more than just completing a piece of writing. It is very important that teachers go through the task carefully with the children so that they know what to do. Clearly not all the children, or parents, will be able to read the instructions in English and so this preparation is crucial if the children are to be able to share the activity. The sheet often acts more as a backup or a prompt than a recipe.

Diaries

The shared writing works by involving parents in their children's learning. The IMPACT diaries* are a crucial part of this process. They provide a mechanism by means of which an efficient parent-teacher-dialogue is established. These diaries enable teachers to obtain valuable feedback both about children's performances in relation to specific activities and about the tasks themselves. Parents are able to alert the teacher to any matter of concern or pleasant occurrences, and nothing is left to come as a big surprise or a horrible shock in the end of year report. It is difficult to exaggerate the importance of the IMPACT diaries. The OFSTED inspectors and HMI have highly commended their effectiveness in helping to raise children's achievements and in developing a real partnership with parents.
* See the Afterword (page 128) for details of where to obtain these.

Timing

Most schools send the Shared Writing activities fortnightly. Many interleave these activities with the IMPACT maths tasks, thus ensuring that the children have something to share with their parents almost every week. Many schools also use the shared writing tasks to enhance their shared reading or PACT programme. It has been found that some parents may be encouraged to take a renewed interest in reading a book with their child on a regular basis when the shared writing project is launched in a class. However, there are a variety of practices and the important point is that each teacher should feel comfortable with how often IMPACT is sent in her class.

Parent friendly

It is important for the success of the IMPACT Shared Writing that parents are aware of both the purpose and the extent of each activity. Many teachers adopt a developmental approach to writing, encouraging emergent writing or the use of invented spellings. Care has to be taken to share the philosophy behind this approach with parents, and to select activities which will not assume that parents are as familiar with the implications as teachers. You will get lots of support if parents can see that what they are doing is helping their child to become cheerful and successful writers!

To facilitate this process, each activity contains a note to parents which helps to make it clear what the purpose of the activity is, and how they can best help. The activities also contain hints to help parents share the activity in an enjoyable and effective manner. Sometimes the hints contain ideas, or starting points. On other occasions they may be examples or demonstrations of how to set about the task concerned.

It is always important to bear in mind that parents can, and sometimes should, do things differently at home. At home, many children will enjoy, and even benefit from, copying underneath a line of text or writing without paying attention to spelling or punctuation, where in school such things might not be expected or encouraged. The most successful partnerships between home and school recognise both the differences and the similarities in each other's endeavours.

Planning

The shared writing activities are divided into four sections according to age: Year 3, Year 4, Year 5 and Year 6. There are two pages of teachers' notes relating to the individual activities at the beginning

of each section. When selecting which activity to send home with the children it is helpful to remember the following:
- Ideally, we send the same activity with each child in the class or year. The activities are mostly designed to be as open-ended as possible, to allow for a wide variety of different levels of response. Teachers often add a few extra comments of their own to a particular sheet to fit it to the needs of a particular child or group of children with special educational needs. It is also important to stress that the child does not have to do all the actual writing – often the parent does half or more. The point of the activity may lie in the discussion and the creation of a joint product.
- It is useful to send a variety of different activities. Some children will particularly enjoy a word game, while others will prefer a task which includes drawing a picture. Activities may be used to launch a topic, to support a particular project, to enable a good quality of follow-up to an idea and to revise or practise particular skills. Much of the benefit of the shared writing exercise may be derived from the follow-up work back in the classroom. Therefore, it is very important to select activities which will feed into the type of work being focused upon at that time. For example, if the class is working on grammatical categories, verbs, nouns, etc., then an activity requiring that children and parents produce real and fictional definitions of long words will fit in well. On the other hand, if the class is doing some work on fairy stories, making a **wanted** poster of a character in a story may be appropriate.

Notes to teachers

These give suggestions to the teachers. They outline what may be done before the activity is sent to ensure that it goes well at home. And they describe how the activity may be followed up as part of routine classwork during the subsequent week. More help with what happens when the activity comes back is to be found in the Afterword on page 128.

Parent letter and booklet

It is very important that parents are kept informed about the nature of this new-style homework. Most schools elect to launch IMPACT Shared Writing by having a meeting or a series of meetings. We have included here a draft letter to parents and a booklet which schools may photocopy and give to parents. The booklet is eight A5 pages when copied, folded and collated. This can be given to all new parents as their children start school. There is a space on the cover for the school name.

Keeping shared writing going...

There are a few tips which have been found over the years to make life simpler for parents, teachers and children:
- Don't send shared writing activities in the first few weeks of the September term. Shared writing, like IMPACT maths, usually starts in the third week of the new school year.
- Don't send shared writing activities in the second half of the summer term. Shared writing, like IMPACT maths, usually belongs to the heart of the school year.
- Do value the work that the children and their parents do at home. Sometimes it may not be presented as you expect – for example, a lot of parents with young children write in upper case rather than lower case letters or will ask children to **write over** a line of print. Remember that what comes back into class is a starting point for work that you consider appropriate, and is facilitating both discussion and partnership.

Dear Parents,

In our class, we have decided to use a new 'shared homework scheme' designed to help develop and improve children's writing skills. This will involve sending home a regular task in the form of an A4 sheet. The sheet will outline a simple writing activity for you and your child to enjoy together. These are designed to be shared; the children are not expected to complete the tasks alone.

We would very much like to talk to you about this scheme, and so on _____ we shall hold three short meetings. You need only come to **one** of these and can choose the time which is most convenient:
- 9.00 in the morning
- 3.30 in the afternoon
- 7.00 in the evening.

We would really like as many parents as possible to attend.

Your help in supporting your child's learning is a crucial part of his/her success at school. We do appreciate the time and trouble that parents take with their children, and we can certainly see the benefits in the quality of the children's work and the enthusiasm with which they attack it.

Please return the slip at the bottom of the letter.

Yours sincerely,

_____

Name _____   Class _____

I would like to attend the meeting at:

9.00 in the morning

3.30 in the afternoon

7.00 in the evening

Please tick **one** time only.

IMPACT

Shared Writing

SPIKE

School name

_____

Don't forget...

Pick your time!
When you both want to do the activity.

Don't over-correct!
This can be very discouraging.

Your child does not always have to do all the writing!
You may take turns, or take over sometimes.

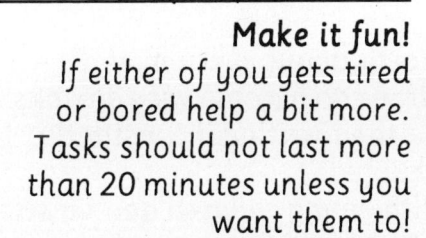

Make it fun!
If either of you gets tired or bored help a bit more. Tasks should not last more than 20 minutes unless you want them to!

Praise and encourage as much as you can!

About Shared Writing

- The teacher selects an activity
- The teacher explains the activity to the class.
- Child and helper read through the activity.
- Child and helper talk about the activity.
- Child and helper share the writing.
- Child and helper comment on the activity in the diary.
- Child brings the activity back into school.
- Teacher reads the comments in the diary.
- The teacher follows up the activity in class.

Spelling and punctuation

We all agree that correct spelling and punctuation are very important. However........

DO

- Notice punctuation when sharing the writing activity.
- Talk about different uses of capital and lower case letters.
- Play word games such as 'I spy' or 'Hangman'.
- Read what the child has written before you make any comment about spelling, punctuation or presentation.
- Help them learn any words sent home by the school.

DON'T

- Worry about every mistake – children can become very anxious about their writing if constantly interrupted.
- With young children don't insist that they spell every word correctly. At this stage we are encouraging them to 'be writers'.
- Don't worry if your child is quite slow to learn to spell and punctuate – these things come with time and encouragement.

How we write

Writing also has a mechanical side, children have to learn to form their letters, to separate words, to begin and end sentences.

When children are first learning to write it can be very discouraging to be constantly corrected. However, as they become more confident, we can afford to draw their attention to these things:

Becoming independent...

As they get older, children need encouragement to become independent readers and writers. But this doesn't mean that there is no role for a supportive parent. In some ways your help is more and not less necessary...

- Talk about the book they are reading – or even comics or magazines etc. This really helps to encourage children to read. Ask questions like:
What do you like about this book?
What exciting things happen? Tell me the story...
Which books are good and which are boring?

- Try to read some of the books your child reads. This really gives you a shared experience – and lots to talk about!

- Help them to become confident and independent spellers...

Don't shout because they spell something wrongly!
Do encourage them by looking for letter patterns.
Don't mock a child who finds spelling hard.
Do make a SHORT list of common words and pin it up in the bathroom where everyone sees it every day!

Being a writer...

Is about...
Having ideas
Composing them
Communicating them

WANTED
A Purpose
a.k.a.
A Greeting
A Compliment
An Enquiry
A Gossip
A Thought

To An Audience
my teacher
mum or Dad
Friend or Foe
Near or Far

Choose from our catalogue of Types of Writing
a letter
a poster
a list
a book

Parents can help by...

Suggesting beginnings...
~~Once upon a time~~
Last night
I went to

Developing characters...
My friend ~~'s~~ Sally's house. Sally is older than me ~~with~~ she likes animals ~~and~~ especially horses

Dear ~~Lizzie~~ ~~Elizabeth~~ ~~Queenie~~ Your Majesty
I would like to...

Developing a sense of style...

and then I...

suggesting ways to end...

Teachers' Notes
YEAR THREE

Table organiser Read through some of the children's ideas. Use one set of instructions, and set up the area as instructed. Can the children understand what to do from the instruction? Talk about the way the children have explained themselves; has anyone used diagrams or illustrations? What is better, to have more words, or less?

The rules of the game Discuss the games for which the children have written rules. Which is the most popular game in the class, or has everyone chosen different games. If possible, test out some of the game rules. Remind the children that they have to imagine that they have never played the game before to test whether the game rules are clear or not. Talk about how different it is to write rules down; what things did the children have to consider when they were working out what to write?

What's outside? Try this activity out at school first; give everyone (including yourself) a piece of paper and a pencil, and sit outside for three minutes making notes. Back inside get the children to write down the things that they saw on a large sheet of paper using their notes. What about things that they heard? Did the children use their notes? When the children bring back their lists, see how similar they are. Use the list as an inspiration for starting stories: 'From my window I could see...'.

The special award Look at the children's certificates; who are they for? Ask a few of the children to explain their certificates to the rest of the class. How have they prepared their certificates? Which ones look the most realistic. Display the certificates in the classroom.

Stranded! Before this activity goes home, talk about the possible situations where people can become stranded. Back in school, ask a few of the children to explain their story and read their note. What kind of information did they choose to put on the note? Did they write short, or long notes? Compare strategies with other children in the class. You could then use the notes as the starting point for a longer piece of imaginative writing.

Hostage teddy Before this activity goes home, talk about the possible situations where you might take a hostage! When the 'ransom notes' come back into school, ask a few of the children to explain their stories and read their notes. What did they put on the note? Did they write short, or long notes? How did they disguise their handwriting? Compare strategies with other children in the class. Use the notes as the starting point for a longer piece of imaginative writing, or some drama work.

Game instructions Go through the game instructions with the children before the activity goes home, just to see if you can discover the missing line of instructions. (There is no way to see how someone wins the cards, and how many cards they win.) Discuss which other games you might be able to write instructions for. 'Snap!' is a very simple game, and yet it is quite difficult even to write instructions for that! Emphasise the fact that they will need to keep to a simple game, or they will get into difficulties very quickly! Try one child's instructions; if you have all the appropriate pieces in school, group the children and try it out.

'Cockles and mussels, alive, alive oh!' Talk through the song in school or even teach it to the children before you send this activity home. This would be a particularly good activity if you have a local market where you will still hear some 'calling'. When the children bring back their calls, ask them to try them out the way they are called out in the market, or wherever they come from. This will be a useful resource for drama and poetry.

'How to open' Look at a few boxes (cereal boxes etc.) to illustrate the instructions you get on packaging, before this activity goes home. Back in school read a few of the children's instructions out, and see if the other children can guess what kind of package they came from. Talk about the range of methods the designers have used to explain what to do. Can the children rewrite their instructions in a clearer way?

Knock knock... 'Knock Knock' jokes often use puns, or plays on part of words to make the jokes funny. Look at a few of the children's jokes, and analyse them – what is it that makes this joke funny? Put all the children's jokes into a class book of jokes that the children can illustrate. Talk about other kinds of puns; can the children think of any more.

New Year resolutions Talk about what a 'resolution' is. You could look it up in the dictionary together. This will be a good activity to send home over the Christmas holiday, or at the start of the Spring Term. When the children bring back the resolutions, talk about the kind of thing they resolved to do/not to do.

Chocolate heaven! Use the information collected as a survey which can then be incorporated into data-handling work in the classroom. Can they design advertising material to go with their new chocolates? Get the children to make posters, with slogans advertising their new product. Who will be most likely to buy their chocolate? Can they aim their advertising at those specific customers.

The best and worst of TV Collect all the children's ratings together, and try to make a kind of 'class chart' (like the music charts) which shows the positioning of all the children's favourite programmes in relation to one another. What kind of programme are the top few in your chart? Are they situation comedy, soap opera, current affairs, educational, comedy or cartoons? What makes them so popular? Design a new programme together that would be watched by the children in your class. Write a list of the components the programme will need, and perhaps design a poster promoting it. If you have access to a video camera, you could even write a 'trailer' for it as well.

Diwali Talk to the children about *why* they are making the cards. Discuss the fact that

impact WRITING HOMEWORK

Writing for a purpose 11

festivals provide us with a reason for greeting each other. Make a list of all the festivals and other occasions, such as birthdays, weddings, deaths, anniversaries – on which we send cards. Make a class display of many different types of cards.

Sweet tooth Before this activity goes home, talk through the reasons why sugar is bad for your teeth; the children should be clear on this before they start their posters. Talk about how you can look after your teeth, and some of the things you can do to prevent decay. If you can, invite a dentist, or oral hygienist to come and talk to the children. Display the posters.

Angry! What does make the children really angry? What *kind* of think makes them angry? Are they concerned about such things as social injustices for example, homelessness, poverty, intolerance and war? Or do they get annoyed by things closer to home: litter, late buses, noisy brothers/sisters, free newspapers, early bedtime, too much homework? The results of this activity should provide a mountain of material to use for some creative writing, and poetry in particular.

These are a few of my favourite things... Make a class list of all the children's favourite things. Classify these under different headings, for example activities, toys, etc. Ask the children to 'rate' their favourite things from 5 down to 1. Make a list of the things which are generally popular and have a vote on which ones are *most* liked. Which activity/outing/toy gets the most votes? Discuss how to record the number of votes each gets. Make a graph or chart to show this.

Where do I go? Before this activity goes home, talk with the children about feeling lost in school when they were only five or six years old. What kind of signs would they have found useful? Ask the children for their stories of their experiences of starting school. When the children bring back their signs, talk about how easy they are to understand. Are they clear, concise and eye-catching. Talk about where you would display the signs; don't forget how tall five and six year olds are!

Best foot forward! Talk through the children's instructions. Read out a few of them and get a volunteer to follow the instructions word for word. Do they end up with their shoes on the right feet? Try writing instructions for other things, for example, if they had to learn to walk again, or operate a computer.

Sandwich maker When the children bring their instructions in, look at the range of ingredients required, and buy enough filling and bread to make a few of the types of sandwiches. Put the children in groups to make the sandwiches; directly following the instructions. What do they come up with? Are they edible? Now cut the sandwiches up into tiny, bite-size pieces. Let everyone have a taste of the sandwiches made. Devise a questionnaire with the children rating the sandwiches on presentation, texture, taste and originality.

Happy birthday to you! Link this activity with other information book-making activities such as Advent calendars or class yearbooks. Look at other sources of information that are sorted by month order such as calendars, weather information, magazine collections and many books about seasonal gardening or cookery. Set the children some sorting and retrieving games and exercises to test their speed against a clock or each other.

Oi! Tidy up your bedroom! Notes and memos like this have a particular function and style. Discuss with children the features of note writing. Provide them with 'Memo Pads'. Get them to leave notes to each other in secret places like the inside of library books (these are called 'dead letters'). Read *The Dead Letter Box* by Jan Mark (Puffin). Look at other forms of note sending, for example, e-mail messages and faxes, if you have the facilities.

Seal of approval More elaborate and intricate initial letter designs can be attempted in class. Exploring the use of them in medieval manuscripts historical records and documents will be interesting. Look as well at contemporary uses on Christmas cards. This activity may be linked to more aesthetic aspects of writing such as handwriting and calligraphy and to other ways of making our mark like signatures, initials and graffiti 'tags'.

We're talking telephone numbers! Look at other sources of information that are sorted by alphabet such as library catalogues, indices of books and maps, encyclopaedia and dictionaries. Set the children some sorting and retrieving games and exercises to test their speed against a clock or each other to improve their alphabetic skills. Use other ways of recording written information for sorting and retrieval, such as computer data bases and spreadsheets.

Nearly new! Look at the writing style in small ads columns for a variety of things like cars, houses and household goods. Children can have fun selling their toy cars or dolls' houses, friends or family in the same style writing. Make a display (you could use newspaper format software) and add photographs.

Talking pages Make some frames in the style of children's comics or teen mags that use this format. Provide speech bubbles so the children have to write an imagined dialogue. Select some incidents from favourite story books in class. Set the children the task of extracting the dialogue from the stories to insert in to speech bubbles to accompany the drawings. Make a display of these.

In *my* day! Identify the distinctive features of report and story writing. Get the children to write reports on school historical events for a school newsletter or journal. Get them to interview parents, grandparents or elderly people and make comparative studies under the theme of 'School in My Day'. Use newspaper format software to publish the children's reports.

Open to persuasion Set the children a series of exercises on writing to persuade, using the distinctions of reason (using logic, evidence or cause and effect conclusions), character (referring to reputable and trusted others) and emotion (appeals others are likely to empathise with on the basis of self interest) to categorise and clarify their arguments. Issues could include increasing pocket money, being allowed to watch late night TV or play video games or being allowed to have a party.

12 Writing for a purpose

impact WRITING HOMEWORK

Table organiser

Pretend that you are going to be the teacher for the day.

You need to organise the painting table ready for the children.

- Write down all the things that you will need to get ready.
- Now write some instructions about what you would like the children to paint.

To the helper:
- Talk about the things you need for painting. What painting equipment will they need, and what will they be painting?
- Organise the instructions into numbered points, that are easy to follow.

Writing instructions requires the children to organise their thoughts clearly, so that another person will understand what they are to do.

_____and
child

_____
helper(s)

_____
did this activity together

impact WRITING HOMEWORK

Writing for a purpose 13

To the helper:

- Talk about the games your child likes to play. Try not to make this task too difficult for yourselves! For example, describing the rules of a ball game might be a lot simpler than attempting a complicated computer game.
- It might be helpful to organise the rules into numbered points.

Writing rules requires the children to organise their thoughts clearly, so that another person will understand what they can do, and what they cannot do.

_____ and
child

_____
helper(s)

_____

did this activity together

14   Writing for a purpose

The rules of the game

What games do you play in the playground, or at home?

What is your favourite game?

- Write down all the rules for the game so that nobody can cheat!

impact WRITING HOMEWORK

What's outside?

- Look out of a window for three minutes.
- Now write down everything that you see.

Can you hear anything that you cannot see?

To the helper:

- Sit together to do this task, but you can each take independent notes on what you see. Do not talk at all for the three minutes. Do you have the same things written down on your pieces of paper? What extra things did you hear?

Children find it very difficult to get started in their writing. This activity helps them to practise taking notes which can then be drawn on for an extended piece of writing at school.

_____ and
child

_____
helper(s)

_____
did this activity together

impact WRITING HOMEWORK

Writing for a purpose 15

To the helper:

- Talk about the people you know who might deserve a certificate.
- Do you have any certificates to look at to give you an idea of what a real one looks like?
- Try to make the design look as realistic as possible.

Designing a certificate makes the children focus on writing in a specific style for a specific purpose.

_____ and
child

_____
helper(s)

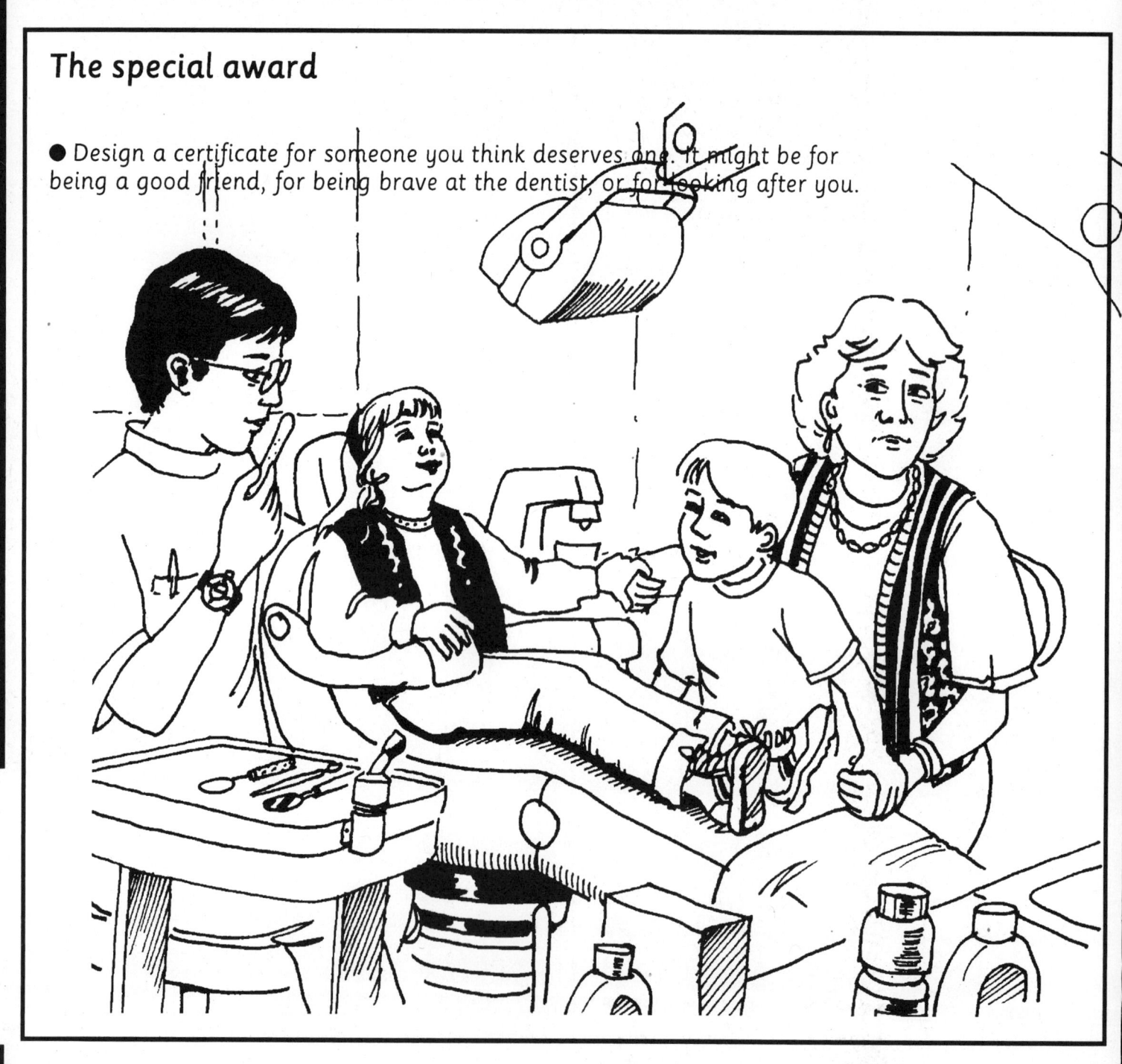

_____
did this activity together

16   Writing for a purpose

The special award

● Design a certificate for someone you think deserves one. It might be for being a good friend, for being brave at the dentist, or for looking after you.

impact WRITING HOMEWORK

Stranded!

Imagine that you are stranded! There is no telephone, but you can send a written message. It could be:
- a message in a bottle
- a message typed on a computer
- a note slipped under a door.

● Imagine your situation, and write down the message you would send.

To the helper:
- This does not have to be a story about a shipwreck; it could be about losing your bus fare for example.
- Talk about the different ways we can send written messages, for example on the computer, by notes etc.
- Remember, keep the message to the point.

Writing short, important messages is an example of writing for a purpose. The children will need to concentrate on the reason for their note in order for the reader to be clear about the situation and to respond accordingly. These ideas will be used as part of an extended writing session at school.

_____and
child

_____
helper(s)

did this activity together

impact WRITING HOMEWORK

Writing for a purpose   17

To the helper:

- Think about the ransom notes you might have seen in books or on the television. How do the authors keep their identity a secret? How many ways can you think of?
- What might the note say? What will the ransom be?

Writing short, important messages is an example of writing for a purpose. The children will need to concentrate on the reason for their note in order for the reader to be clear about the situation and how to respond. These notes will be used as part of an extended writing session at school.

_____ and
child

_____
helper(s)

_____
did this activity together

18   Writing for a purpose

Hostage teddy

Imagine that you have taken someone's teddy bear hostage!

You will need to write a ransom note that does not show your handwriting.

● Design a suitable note that would keep your identity a secret.

impact WRITING HOMEWORK

Game instructions

What games do you play in the playground, or at home?

What is your favourite game?

- Try playing this card game called 'Snap!' using these instructions:

- Try these instructions out, are there any missing?

- Write down the instructions for a different game so that no-one can cheat at it.

How to play 'Snap!', a game for two players or more.

You will need:
a pack of cards.

1. Deal all of one pack of cards equally between all players. Everyone holds their cards in a pile facing down.
2. Player to the left of the dealer starts by placing a card face up on the table.
3. Next player to the left does the same, and so on. If two cards are played one after the other, that are the same number, players must all shout 'Snap!' as soon as they notice.
4. If a player plays all their cards they are still in the game until someone else beats them by shouting 'Snap!' first, and takes their cards from the table. Play continues until one player wins all the cards.

To the helper:

- Read out the instructions for the game very carefully together to notice if any are missing while you play.
- Talk about the rules in your game; are there any that you have made up yourselves?
- This activity will require quite a lot of writing, so take over if necessary.

This activity will make the children think very carefully about what they write, and how they write it. Back in the classroom we shall try out everyone's game instructions to see if they are clear and easy to understand.

_____ and
child

_____
helper(s)

_____
did this activity together

impact WRITING HOMEWORK

Writing for a purpose   19

To the helper:

- Talk about the sort of things these people call out; are they always easy to understand?

Recording information is an important skill in writing. The children will be sharing their 'calls' at school.

_____ and
child

_____
helper(s)

_____
did this activity together

'Cockles and mussels, alive, alive oh!'

This line comes from a song about a girl called Molly Malone who sold cockles and mussels. This was her cry to attract customers.

What do people call now?

● Write down one thing that is called out by:
- market traders
- train guards
- newspaper sellers.

20 **Writing for a purpose**

impact WRITING HOMEWORK

'How to open'

Many boxes, cartons, bottles, and even bags come with special 'How to open' instructions.

- Hunt through some packaging at home, and see what you can find.

- Write down the most complicated set of instructions you can find. Do not write down where they came from – we shall try and guess at school!

To the helper:

- Look for a suitably complicated set of instructions together in your home.
- Talk about the different way instructions are given; through diagrams, pictures, numbered points as well as writing.

This activity focuses the children's attention on the ways instructions are given in a variety of situations. Being able to follow, and write instructions is an important skill.

_____and

child

_____

helper(s)

did this activity together

impact WRITING HOMEWORK

Writing for a purpose

To the helper:

- Tell one another the 'Knock Knock' jokes that you both know. Does your child understand why the jokes are funny? They are usually a play on words.
- How easy is it to write down the joke without either spelling it wrongly, or giving away the joke?

Back at school, we shall tell one another the jokes, and discuss what makes the jokes funny. We shall look more closely at puns, and the way the English language can at one time be confusing, and at others, funny!

_____and
child

_____
helper(s)

_____
did this activity together

22   Writing for a purpose

Knock Knock...

Do you know any 'Knock Knock' jokes?

- Write down one that you know.

impact WRITING HOMEWORK

New Year resolutions

What did you resolve to do or not do this year?

If you did not make a New Year's resolution, what **could** you have decided on?

- Write down a New Year's resolution.

To the helper:

- Talk about what it means to make a New Year's resolution. It is about starting the year as you mean to go on. A chance to make a fresh start symbolically.

Writing resolutions provides the children with a reason for writing. We shall talk about our New Year resolutions back at school.

_____and
child

_____
helper(s)

_____
did this activity together

impact WRITING HOMEWORK   Writing for a purpose   23

To the helper:

- Talk about the vast range of chocolate that is available, including chocolate bars, chocolate-covered bars, and fancy chocolates in boxes!
- Try to think up a new type of chocolate with an irresistible name.

Writing chocolate names, and inventing new ones, provides the children with a reason for writing. We shall talk about our chocolates back at school.

_____ and
child

_____
helper(s)

_____
did this activity together

24   Writing for a purpose

Chocolate heaven!

There are many, many different types of chocolate.

Which is your favourite kind?

- Write the name of your favourite kind of chocolate.
- Now invent a whole new brand of chocolate.
- Write down its name and describe it too.

impact WRITING HOMEWORK

The best and worst of TV

- Think of five programmes that you watch.

You are going to give five stars to the best one (as far as you are concerned); and one star to the worst.

- Arrange your five programmes in order from five stars to one star (best to worst).

For example:

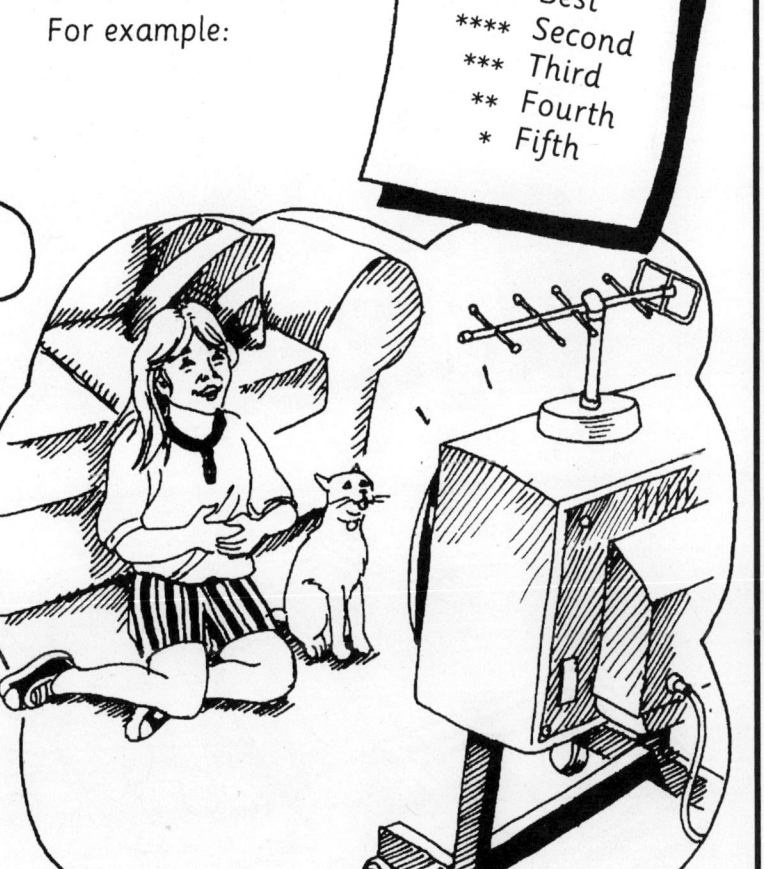

```
***** Best
****  Second
***   Third
**    Fourth
*     Fifth
```

To the helper:
- Talk about the programmes that your child watches the most. Do they ever express an opinion about them?
- Ask your child what they like about the different programmes, and what they do not like.

Rating the children's programmes requires the children to consider why they do or do not like a programme, and to express their opinions. They are also given a purpose for writing down the information. We shall be discussing the children's viewing preferences at school.

_____and
child

_____
helper(s)

_____
did this activity together

impact WRITING HOMEWORK

Writing for a purpose 25

To the helper:

- Diwali is a festival that is shared by both Sikhs and Hindus. The festival is very ancient and, like other festivals around the same time, it concerns the power and imagery of lights shining in the darkness.

Making cards for festivals such as Christmas, Easter, Hannukah and Diwali provides a real purpose for both writing and drawing.

_____and
child

_____
helper(s)

did this activity together

26 **Writing for a purpose**

Diwali

- Make a card for someone celebrating Diwali.

What message might you write inside?

- Bring the card to school.

impact WRITING HOMEWORK

Sweet tooth

- Design a poster that might help people think twice about eating sweets.

To the helper:
- Talk about the reasons why you should not eat too many sweets, and why you should take care of your teeth.
- What kinds of words and phrases should appear on the poster?

Making posters is one type of writing for a purpose. Information has to be communicated in an attractive, eye-catching and clear way. We shall display and talk about the posters at school.

_____and
child

_____
helper(s)

_____
did this activity together

impact WRITING HOMEWORK

Writing for a purpose 27

To the helper:

- Talk about the things that irritate, annoy or just enrage your child.
- Put the things in order, from 1 most annoying → 5 least annoying.

Recording information is an important purpose for writing. We shall be discussing things that make the children angry at school.

_____ and
child

_____
helper(s)

_____
did this activity together

28 **Writing for a purpose**

Angry!

- Write down five things that make you really angry.

impact WRITING HOMEWORK

These are a few of my favourite things...

What brings a smile to your face?

- Write down five things.

To the helper:

- Talk about the things that make your child happy, or amuses them.
- Put the things in order, from 1 most amusing → 5 least amusing.

Recording information is an important purpose for writing. We shall be discussing things that make the children smile at school.

_____ and
child

_____
helper(s)

_____
did this activity together

impact WRITING HOMEWORK

Writing for a purpose 29

To the helper:

- Discuss what it was like for your child to be an Infant, and how easy it is to get lost in a school.
- Think of a particular place together which an Infant may need to find and decide what kind of sign will be easiest for very young children to 'read'.

Writing signs will help children be clear and concise about what they write. It helps them to learn to use precise language.

_____and
child

_____
helper(s)

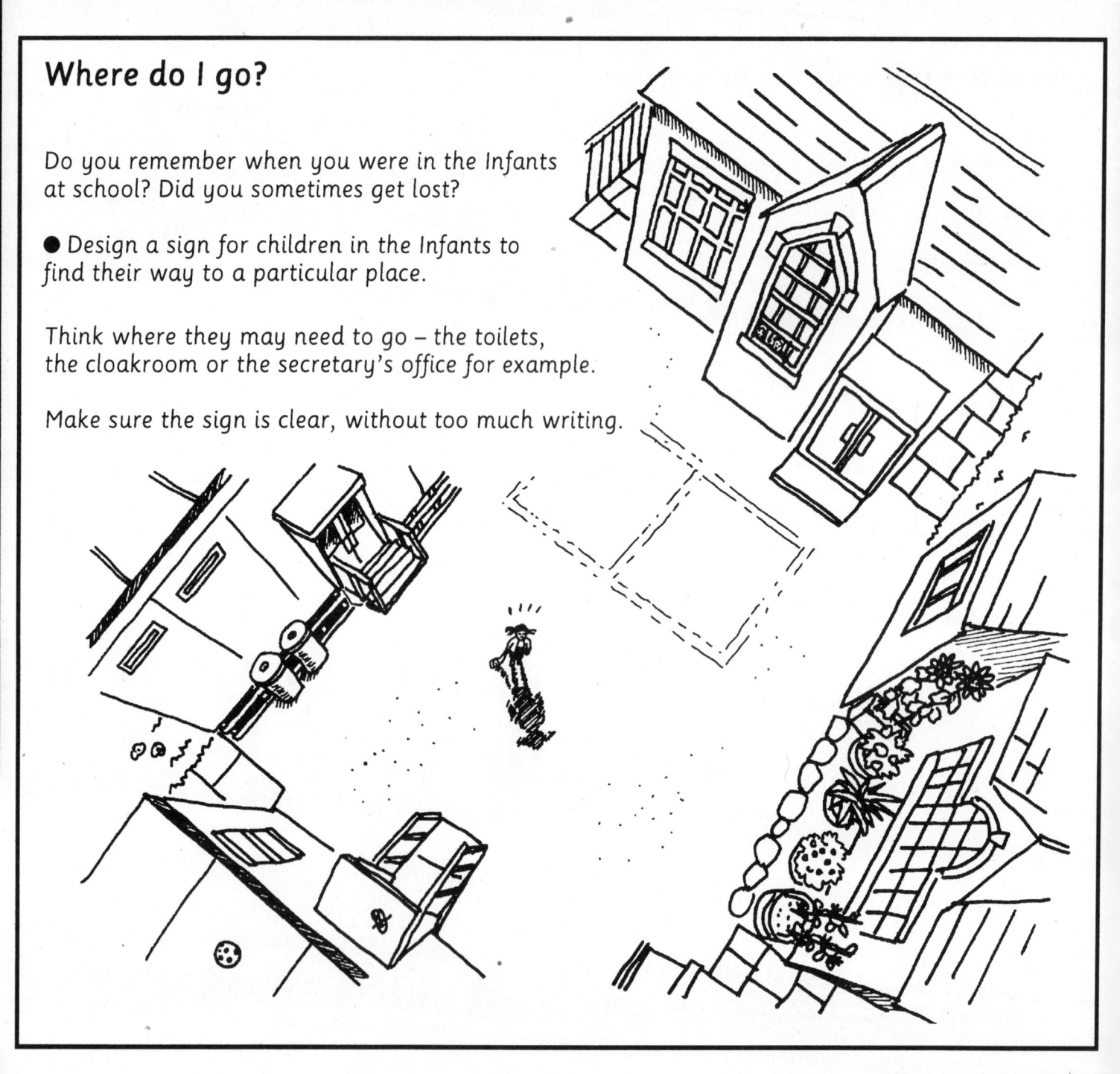

did this activity together

Where do I go?

Do you remember when you were in the Infants at school? Did you sometimes get lost?

● Design a sign for children in the Infants to find their way to a particular place.

Think where they may need to go – the toilets, the cloakroom or the secretary's office for example.

Make sure the sign is clear, without too much writing.

30   **Writing for a purpose**

impact WRITING HOMEWORK

Best foot forward!

How do you put your shoes on? Can you explain?

● Write some instructions for a child learning how to put their shoes on. You may use diagrams if you want!

To the helper:

● It might help to actually go through the stages of putting a pair of shoes on with your child. You can pretend to be the younger child and they will have to give you the instructions. This will help them to think it through before they write it down.

This activity will make the children think very carefully about what they write, and how they write it. Back in the classroom we shall try out everyone's instructions to see if they are clear and easy to understand.

_____and
child

_____
helper(s)

_____
did this activity together

impact WRITING HOMEWORK

Writing for a purpose 31

To the helper:

- Talk about the type of sandwich that is your child's favourite. Do they ever make their own sandwiches?
- Discuss how you will set out the information so that it is clear.

This activity will make the children think very carefully about what they write, and how they write it. Back in the classroom we shall try out a few of the instructions to see if they are clear and easy to understand.

_____ and

child

_____

helper(s)

_____

did this activity together

Sandwich maker

What kind of sandwich is your favourite?

● Write some instructions for someone else to make your favourite sandwich for you.

32   **Writing for a purpose**

impact WRITING HOMEWORK

Happy birthday to you!

- Make a birthday and anniversary diary so that you won't forget the important dates of family and friends. Arrange them by month order.

To the helper:
- Help your child by listing the family and friends who will go into the book. Write the months along the top of a piece of paper for ease of sorting the list.
- Make a little book by folding some paper and stapling or sewing the edge. If you like, cut steps into the edge of the pages to show the months.

Recording information, sorting and retrieving it easily is one of the main purposes of writing. The more children can relate this to their own needs the more they will come to see how writing can enhance the functioning of their lives.

_____ and
child

_____
helper(s)

_____
did this activity together

impact WRITING HOMEWORK

Writing for a purpose

To the helper:

- Talk about all the jobs that have to be done in the house and who does them. This is intended to be fun, so make sure the message is jokey and doesn't start any arguments!

Sometimes leaving a written message for someone is a more powerful way of making your point. Personal notes and memos can be an effective way of communicating, even when joking.

_____ and
child

_____
helper(s)

_____

did this activity together

Oi! Tidy up your bedroom!

Do you get fed up of being reminded of your duties around the house? Here's a chance to remind someone else of theirs!

- Write a note to someone in your house about something they have forgotten to do, for example, leave a note on your parents' bedroom door saying 'Oi! Look at that mess! No watching TV until it's tidied up!' Make sure you leave it where they will notice it.

34 **Writing for a purpose**

impact WRITING HOMEWORK

Seal of approval

Hundreds of years ago people used Personal Seals to show their authority and identify themselves on letters and documents.

● Design a Personal Seal of your own with your initials on it. You can draw it on paper or cut one from a vegetable and print with it using paint or ink or even sealing wax if you have it.

To the helper:

● Help your child design their initials in an interesting and attractive way (you may have seen some decorated initial letters used in manuscripts from medieval times). Try to be as intricate and as colourful as possible. Remind children not to use knives without your supervision.

Learning to 'make our mark' through the written medium is an important way of expressing our individuality and identity.

_____ and
child

_____
helper(s)

_____
did this activity together

impact WRITING HOMEWORK

Writing for a purpose 35

To the helper:

- Help your child by listing the friends who will go into the book. Write the alphabet along the top of a piece of paper for ease of sorting the list.
- Make a little book by folding some paper and stapling or sewing the edge. If you like, cut steps into the edge of the pages to show the letters.

Recording information, sorting and retrieving it easily is one of the main purposes of writing. The more children can relate this to their own needs the more they will come to see how writing can enhance the functioning of their lives.

_____and

child

_____

helper(s)

_____

did this activity together

36 **Writing for a purpose**

We're talking telephone numbers!

● Make a telephone book of your friends' telephone numbers (and relatives' as well if you like) and arrange them in alphabetic order.

impact WRITING HOMEWORK

Nearly new!

- Can you write an ad to sell a member of your family! Say some nice things but be truthful, if that's possible!

To the helper:
- Have a look at the personal ads in your local newspapers or magazines. Help your child choose some selling phrases that will fit the person you want to 'sell'. Try to make it as funny as you can. Use some abbreviations if you like, such as 'gsoh' (good sense of humour).

Personal ads have acquired a particular cryptic style which is unique to the context in which they appear. Learning to write cryptic but accurate and appealing messages is the great skill of advertising copy writers.

_____and
child

_____
helper(s)

_____
did this activity together

impact WRITING HOMEWORK

Writing for a purpose 37

To the helper:

- Help your child find pictures of people they know/like. Look at some magazines. Choose two very different people to make it more funny.
- Spend some time talking about ideas before you stick the things on the paper. Make it look as though a conversation is going on.

This activity helps children think about what people say and how they respond in dialogue. It also focuses on forms of writing that depend on dialogue, such as plays. It is a useful introduction to the use of speech marks in prose.

_____and

child

_____

helper(s)

_____

did this activity together

Writing for a purpose

Talking pages

Find an old newspaper or magazine that has been finished with and has photographs of famous people in it.

- Cut out some pictures and stick them on a piece of paper. Cut out these speech bubbles, stick them on your picture and write a funny dialogue between the characters.

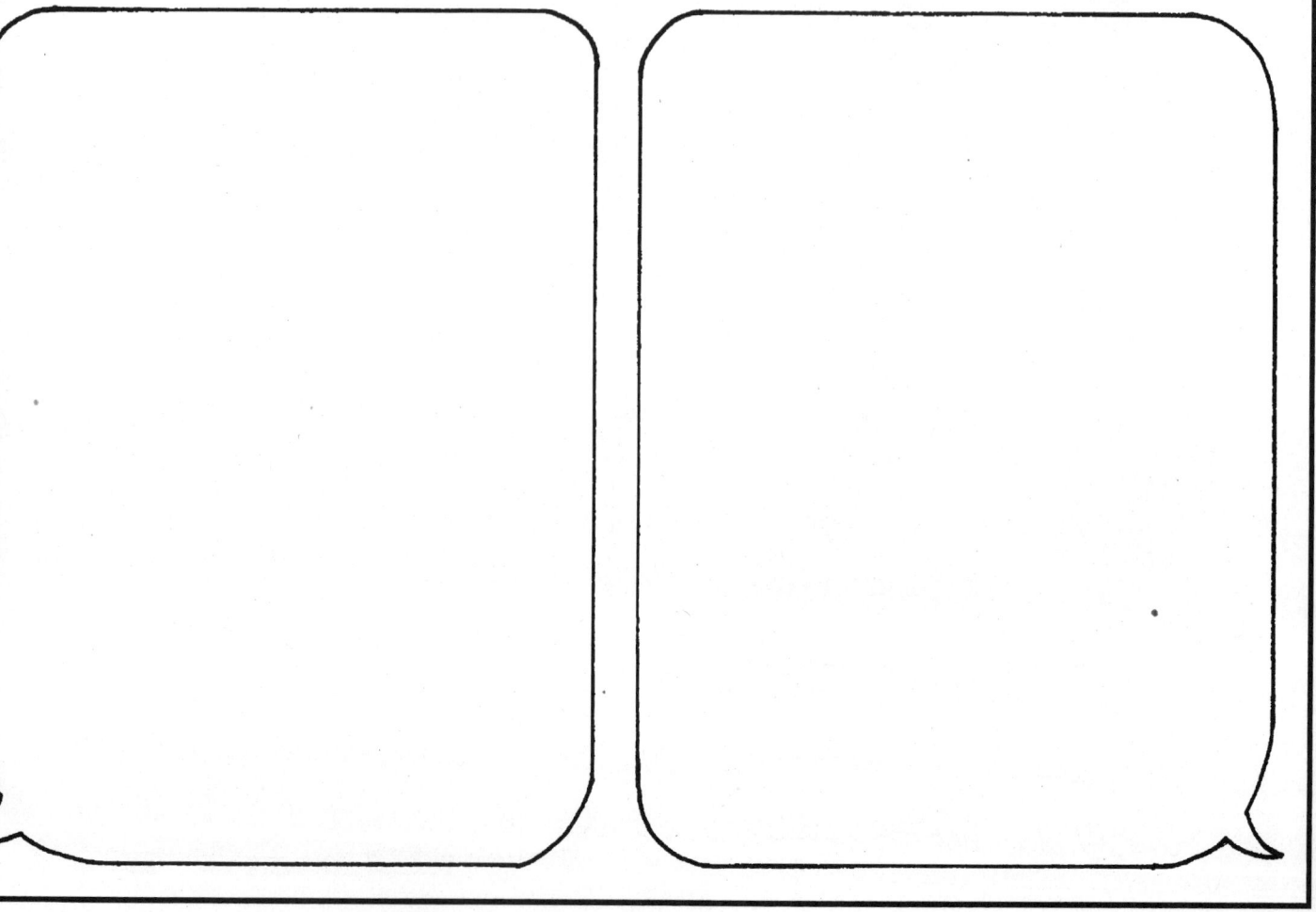

impact WRITING HOMEWORK

In my day!

What was the most memorable thing your mum or dad ever did in school? Get them to tell you about it.

- Write it down together as a report.

To the helper:

- Start by reminiscing about your own school days. Share stories about scoring a goal for a school sports team, getting in trouble with a teacher, adventures on a school outing or winning a school prize. Try to remember one which is dramatic or funny. Let your child write as much as possible as if they were reporting it as an 'Historical Correspondent'.

Writing is an important medium to report incidents across time and space. This activity helps children realise that memories can be preserved when written down.

_____and
child

_____
helper(s)

_____

did this activity together

impact WRITING HOMEWORK

Writing for a purpose

To the helper:

● Help your child think of three different persuasive arguments; one based on *reason* ('Staying up later allows more time to read'), one based on *character* ('Dad stays up late') and one based on *emotion* ('Everybody in my class stays up later than me, it's not fair!'). Design an imaginative way of presenting the argument persuasively, for example using drawings or speech bubbles.

Using writing to persuade is an important skill because through writing, people often contemplate and consider argument more carefully.

_____and
child

_____
helper(s)

_____
did this activity together

Open to persuasion

Do your mum and dad sometimes say 'No!'?

● Write down two or three points that you would use to persuade your mum or dad to allow you to do something you are not normally allowed to do (for example, to let you stay up later than usual).

40 **Writing for a purpose**

impact WRITING HOMEWORK

Teachers' Notes
YEAR FOUR

Post it! Before sending the activity home, buy some adhesive stickers and attach one or two to each child's sheet. In class, discuss what things are always being forgotten. How can we use stickers to remember things in class like timetable, work, or tidying up routines? What other methods are useful as reminders?

'Doctor, doctor...' Before sending the activity home ensure the children are familiar with these jokes. Share some in class. Make a 'Joke of the Day' display board and show a different joke each day. Make a joke book of different kinds of jokes: Doctor, doctor...; Knock, knock! and Why did the chicken cross the road?

Local hero Ask the children to write an encyclopaedia entry for their heroic figures. What is heroism? Where did the notion originate? Has it changed over time? Who were the heroes of a century or ten years ago? The children can go on to paint a portrait of their heroic figures and write newspaper reports of their heroic deed.

Neighbours Make a class list of the questions the children think it would be interesting to ask their neighbours. Talk about surveys – how the questions arise out of the agenda of the people commissioning the survey. Perhaps you can use your list of questions to carry out a class survey. When everyone has answered you will need to collate the results and then analyse them. How will you report back these results? The children can write about what they have discovered – or they can produce a graph or chart.

Babysitter Make inventories of 'Things for Baby' and sort them into essential/non-essential; edible/non-edible; playthings/non-playthings. Invite in new mums to demonstrate bathing, clothing or changing a young baby. Display pictures of the children in your class (and staff) as babies. Organise a guessing game; the children have to submit written guesses matching numbered photos to names. Write 'When I was a baby...' stories.

Mugshots Make a class book including all the descriptions written and mounted on paper under the heading 'Guess Who?'. Underneath (behind a flap) or on the next page put the identity or better still, a photo of a child. Draw around an OHP silhouette and mount black on white for maximum impact. Photograph each other face on and in profile. Display a 'Rogues Gallery'.

'An apple a day...' Draw and paint 'healthy dinner plates' and display them with captions as in some fast food restaurants. Explore nutrition and find out about the relative value of fats, carbohydrates, proteins, vitamins and water. Make a 'Healthy Eating' Board Game; include 'healthy' and 'non-healthy' squares to advance you or send you back.

Postcard message Buy a pack of white postcards and give one out to each child. When they come back, post the cards and map out the various places they have been sent on maps, atlases and globes. Make a display of postcards from far away places. Write some more in class. Each child chooses another to send their card to (make sure each child gets one!). Send these so that each child receives a card in the post.

Exciting foods Write the story of 'The Journey of a Banana' from plantation to fruit bowl. Have a blindfold exotic fruit-tasting or texture-feeling competition and choose unusual fruits like coconuts, guava, sharon, kiwi, star, mangoes or papaya if they are available in your area. Give children a supermarket carrier bag with various exotic foods, herbs and spices and map their origins on photocopied maps of the world. Contact Oxfam Education, for materials and activities on the political economy of food production.
Oxfam Education, 274 Banbury Road, Oxford OX2 7DZ.

Many happy returns/Merry Christmas! Read through a few examples of birthday cards with the children before the activity goes home. Suggest that some of the rhymes could be funny or serious. They could be for a sister, brother, mother, father or grandparent etc. When the rhymes come back into class, make them into cards. How many different ways of making a card can your class come up with? (Pop-up, pull-out, lift-the-flap or zigzag for example.)

This is your life! Bring in a picture of yourself, or a famous person, and write a range of captions for it together. They could be serious or humorous. Encourage the children to think of a few ideas. When the children bring in their own pictures and captions. Make a display of them; has anyone used speech bubbles, or any other captioning techniques?

Musical words Discuss the children's favourite songs. Ask them to write out the words of a favourite song – or a poem – and to decorate their piece of writing with images which give a sense of the music as well as the meaning of the words. Talk about how words, music and images or pictures can all express the same emotions in different ways.

The sound of music Display the results of the surveys of favourite kinds of music, favourite instruments, musicians etc. in graphs, bar and pie charts. Discuss other generational aspects of culture like clothes fashion, hairstyles, dance and how these are often associated with styles of music. Research attitudes to music in history, for example, the Nazis banned jazz and religious people in America said rock and roll was 'the devil's music'.

Model instructions Before sending the activity home, demonstrate to the children

impact WRITING HOMEWORK

Writing for a purpose 41

how to write instructions for a variety of simple tasks like putting batteries in a torch. Set them tasks of writing instructions for the assembly of some simple kits using 'blown' diagrams to complement the writing. Fold an A4 sheet of paper into six panels and set the children the task of instructing someone to 'Make a dolls' house/ spaceship in six simple steps!'.

Just my cup of tea Set the children other tasks of writing procedures that require a sequence, like making a milk shake, a natural lemonade or an egg-nog. Do some research on tea and tea drinking around the world. Find out where it comes from. Map the origins of various teas. Write the 'Story of a tea leaf' from its origins on a bush through to its destination in a tea bag. Contact Oxfam Education for materials on the political economy of tea production. What are the different ways people 'take tea'? Organise a blindfolded tasting with various teas and herbal teas. Oxfam Education, 274 Banbury Road, Oxford OX2 7DZ.

Looking for work! Buy a pack of white postcards and give one to each child to make their final advert on. Design and make postcard size adverts for other casual jobs which children might like to do when they get a little older. Include relevant qualifications, experience and skills. Write a simple CV. Write about career aspirations and life ambitions. Ask the children to consider what qualifications, experience and skills they think they will need.

School signs Design and write some welcome posters for the classroom and school. Have a competition for the most attractive and welcoming. Write in languages other than English if you have children or staff who speak another language. Design and write some functional signs in the classroom and school which use only symbols to direct people. Some signs and symbols are like gestures in writing. Explore gestures in conversation and in performance (like mime).

Road safety campaign Before sending this home discuss slogans of all kinds. Show children a variety of posters with slogans. Talk about the short, cryptic nature of them. Choose the best to enlarge and paint. Make a display of them against windows visible from outside. If you can afford it, colour photocopy a selection for maximum impact. Write to RoSPA, Cannon House, The Priory, Queensway, Birmingham, B4 6BS and ask for some posters and material on preventing road accidents.

Message in a bottle Make a display of a variety of shaped and old bottles with the messages inside them. Make a wall display of a desert island with your faded and crinkled messages (lightly bake them in an oven for effect). Encourage the children to write a list of toys or books that they would take with them or 'Ten essential items for survival on a desert island'.

Magic beans Tell the story of Jack and the Beanstalk (or similar) before sending this activity home. Let the children examine some real (dried!) beans. Write 'Magic Bean' stories, discuss a variety of beginnings, scenarios and endings. What about 'Magic Baked Beans!' stories. Write and prepare some 'Magic Bean Recipes'.

This is how you write a letter... Set the children the task of making a template to fit over an A4 size sheet with cut out spaces for name, address, greeting, introduction etc. in the right places. Play a class game where the children guide a blindfolded child with verbal instructions to place each line of the name, address, introduction, sign-off etc. on to a large prepared letter. Compare the layout of business letters with personal ones.

Media slogan Make a class display of all the slogans with accompanying posters to illustrate them. Make a list of some of the words and concepts used in advertising. Which concepts are 'positive' in some contexts and 'negative' in others. For example safe/exciting or cheap/ expensive. Look at these sets of opposites. Which ones are commonly used? Which ones are never used?

Front page news You may already use class 'news-time' to model report-writing in journalistic styles with a characteristic emphasis on dramatic events and content. Give children time to explore this style further by making a collection of local and national newspaper front pages, especially those in tabloid format. Set the children the task of inventing alliterative headlines for imaginary events in school 'Headteacher hunts for hairy ham sandwich thief!'.

Atlas of my world Drawing and labelling maps and aerial views of all kinds is an important precursor to work on mathematical scale and geographical concepts. Set the children tasks of drawing and labelling maps and plans of their classroom, bedroom or locations in their story books (a map of Narnia for example). These could be the basis of scale models made with paper, card or balsa wood.

Please Miss! Compare the clarity and impact of some arguments compared to others in the samples that are returned. Which ones draw on evidence to support them and which are purely emotive? Set the children other discussion points or issues around which they have to construct points of argument for and against.

Send out for pizza! Before sending the activity home, show the children a range of junk mail leaflets and discuss the techniques of advertising used. Make a display of the leaflets the children produce alongside authentic ones. If you have the facilities or can afford it, choose the best ones to colour photocopy for display, the impact will be stunning. Set the children tasks of calculating the variations, combinations and permutations of pizza or ice cream toppings available from one outlet. Can you make pizza boxes which insulate heat? Design logos and slogans to go on them.

The image of music Before sending the activity home, listen to a piece of music together (you will need to make a careful choice) and talk about the images it may evoke and ask the children to draw a picture as they are listening. Invent new ways of notating music. Use symbols like flat shapes (triangles, squares, circles etc.) to represent the sounds of instruments or body sounds (like mouth pops, claps, clicks etc.). Display notions of 3D shapes to represent various instruments or sounds (like toilet-roll cylinders for swishing noises or cereal boxes for crunching sounds).

Writing for a purpose

impact WRITING HOMEWORK

Post it!

Are there some things which you are always forgetting to do?

● Write yourself a reminder on your sticky label and stick it where you will see it, for example on the front door, on your mirror, or on your school bag.

Does it work? Write down your message, and why you needed to write it and bring it to school.

To the helper:

● Talk about the kinds of things your child is always forgetting to do. Which words would you write on the note? Would one word be sufficient to remind you, or would you need a whole sentence?

Writing messages or reminder notes to ourselves is one of the ways that writing is used in everyday life. We shall talk about our messages, and how effective they were back at school.

_____and
child

_____
helper(s)

_____
did this activity together

impact WRITING HOMEWORK

Writing for a purpose 43

To the helper:

- Tell one another the 'Doctor, doctor...' jokes that you both know. Does your child understand why the jokes are funny? They are often a play on words.
- How easy is it to write down the joke without either spelling it wrongly, or giving away the joke?

Back at school, we shall tell one another the jokes, and discuss what makes the jokes funny. We shall look more closely at puns, and the way the English language can at one time be confusing, and at others funny!

_____ and
child

_____
helper(s)

did this activity together

'Doctor, doctor...'

Do you know any 'Doctor, doctor...' jokes?

- Write down one that you know.

44 **Writing for a purpose**

impact WRITING HOMEWORK

Local hero

Do you know a real-life hero or heroine?

What made them a hero or heroine?

- Write down their name, and how they were heroic.

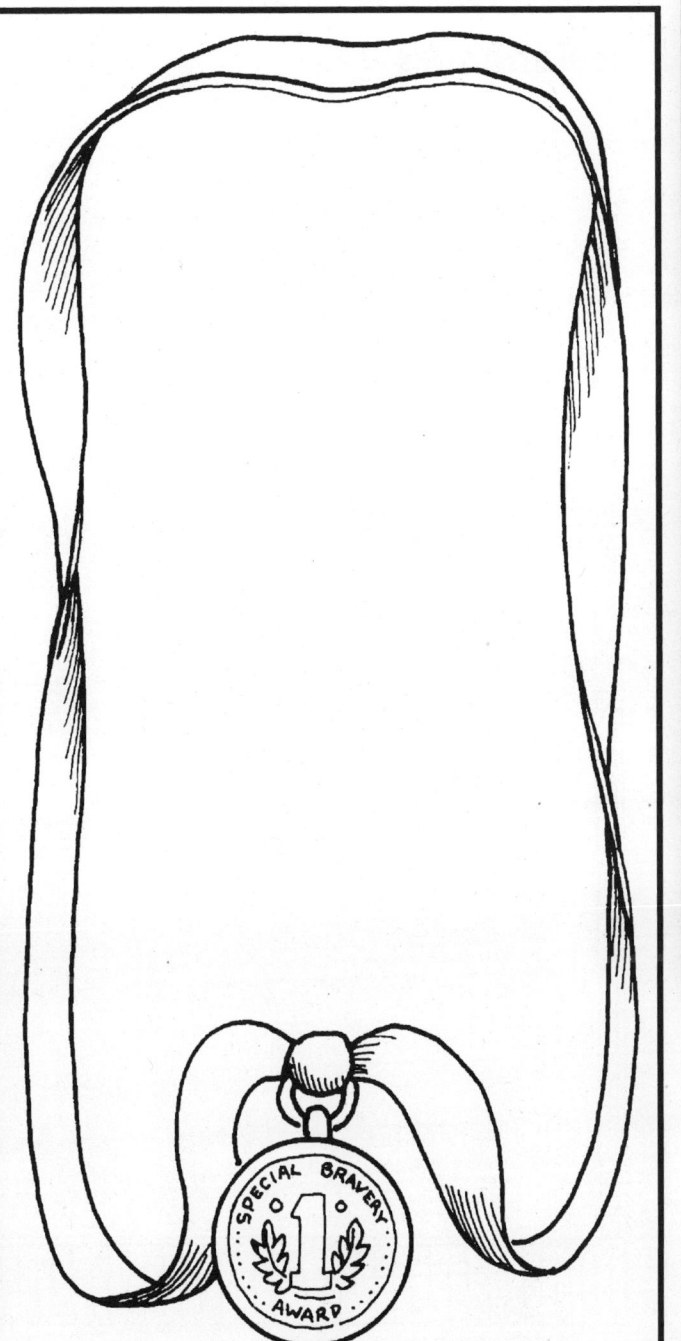

To the helper:

- You do not have to be famous to be heroic. This activity is about identifying heroic characteristics in everyday people. Perhaps you know of someone who had to make some kind of sacrifice for someone else, or put their own safety at risk for someone else, or someone who just always seems to put other people first.

By having to find out about, and then write down the story of a local hero, the children are having to record useful information that we shall be using in the class for further written work.

_____ and
child

_____
helper(s)

_____
did this activity together

impact WRITING HOMEWORK

Writing for a purpose   45

To the helper:

- Talk about your neighbours; what are the kinds of things you say about them at home?
- Perhaps they have strange habits that you have never really understood, like sitting in their car with the engine running for ten minutes before they actually go. Why do they do that?

By having to find out about, and then write down the questions for their neighbours, the children are having to record information that we shall be using in the class for further written work.

_____ and
child

_____
helper(s)

did this activity together

Writing for a purpose

Neighbours

Do you know who your neighbours are?

- What questions would you like to ask them?
- Write down your questions, and bring them into school.

impact WRITING HOMEWORK

Babysitter

What kinds of things do babies need?

- Write down five things you might need if you were going to help someone look after a baby for an afternoon.

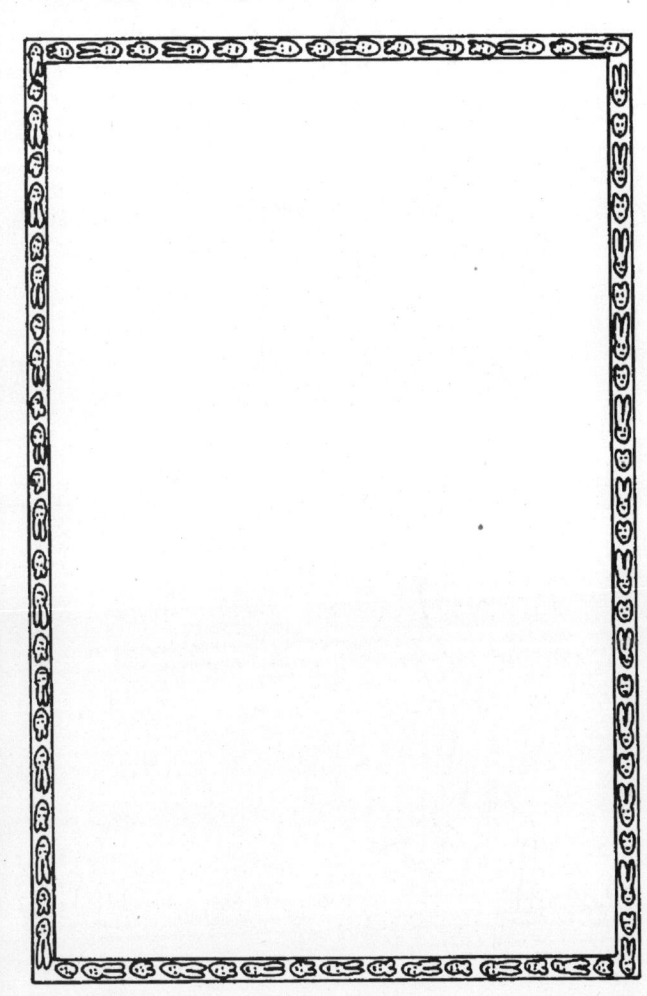

To the helper:

- Talk about the needs of a baby. Do you have a baby in your family, or do you know someone with a baby? Perhaps your child could interview someone who has a baby to collect their information. If not, can you remember all the things that you needed when your child was a baby?

By having to find out about, and then write down the things that a baby might need, the children are having to record useful information that we shall be using in the class for further written work.

_____ and
child

_____
helper(s)

_____
did this activity together

impact WRITING HOMEWORK

Writing for a purpose 47

To the helper:

- Carefully go through all the features of your child's face. It might help to imagine that you are describing their face to someone on the other end of a telephone.
- Talk about the shape of the face, the colour and texture of the skin. The colour, shape and size of the eyes, the eyebrows, eyelashes, the nose and mouth.

By having to examine closely, and write down a description of their face in minute detail, the children are recording useful information that we shall use in the class for further written work.

_____and

child

_____

helper(s)

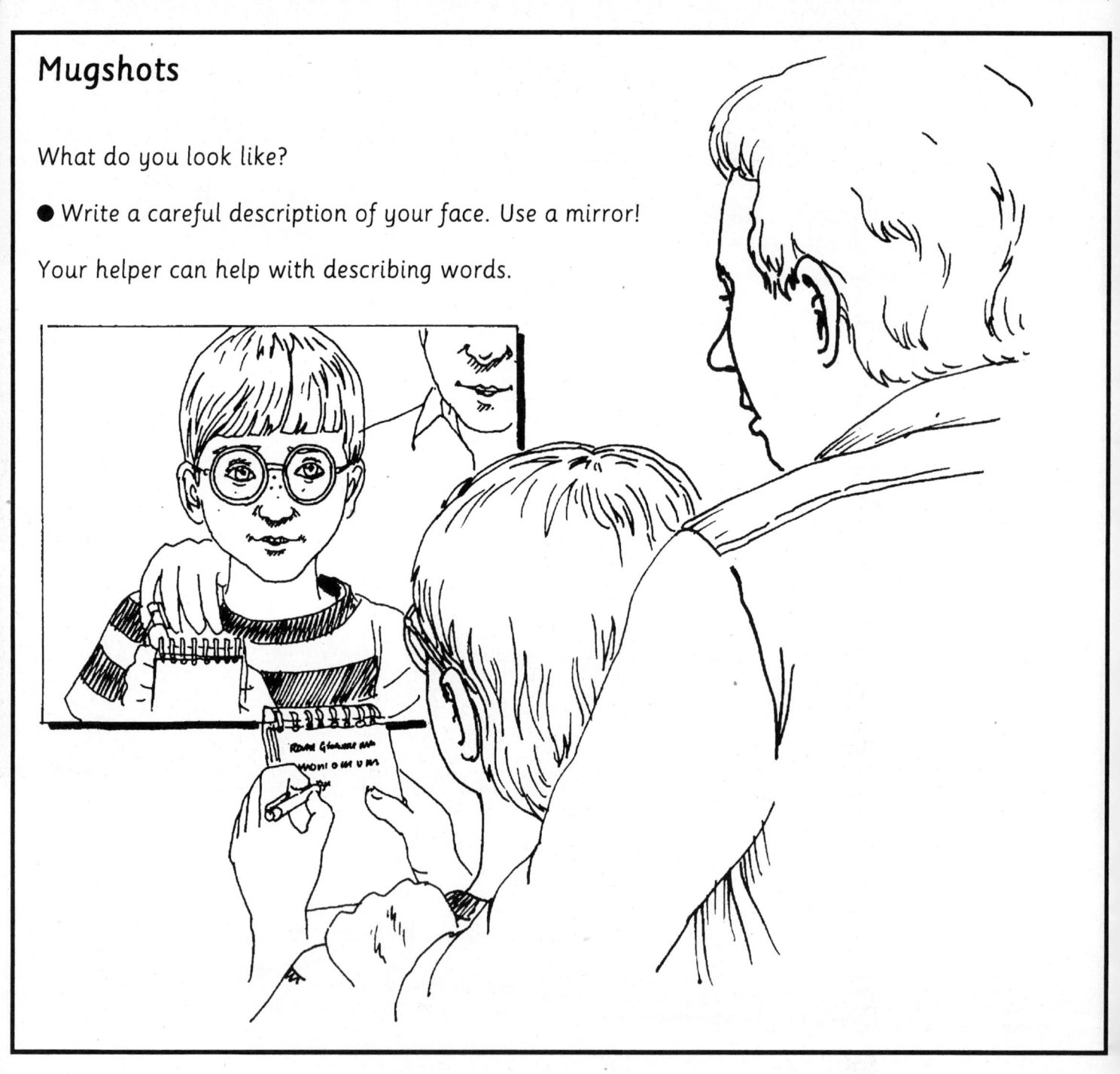

_____

did this activity together

Mugshots

What do you look like?

- Write a careful description of your face. Use a mirror!

Your helper can help with describing words.

48   **Writing for a purpose**

impact WRITING HOMEWORK

'An apple a day...'

- List five things that you can do to keep yourself healthy.

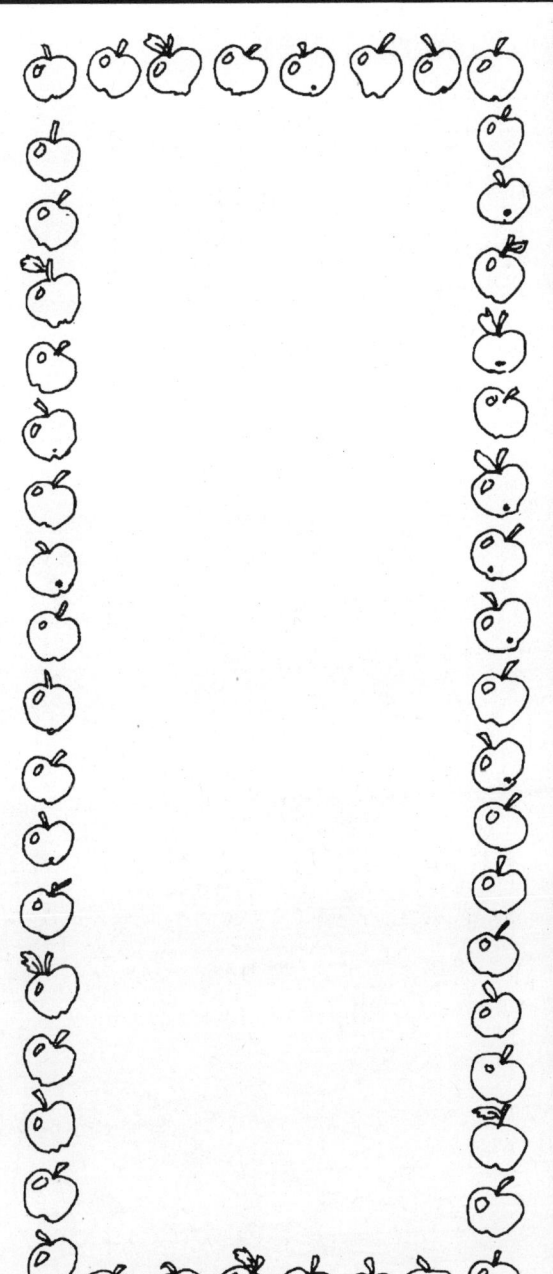

To the helper:

- Talk about the things your child actually does do, and the things he or she could do. For example, eating healthily (lots of fruit and vegetables every day), exercising regularly, not eating crisps and sweets at breaktime, always brushing teeth in the morning and evening.

Writing lists is an important skill which will be useful to the children in several areas of their life in the future. We shall use the list of healthy habits that the children thought of in the class.

_____ and
child

_____
helper(s)

_____

did this activity together

impact WRITING HOMEWORK

Writing for a purpose 49

To the helper:

● Talk to your child about who they could send the postcard to. Discuss what picture they should draw on the front.

Postcards and letters provide a real-life context for writing. We shall be working on the conventions associated with writing these in class.

_____and
child

_____
helper(s)

_____
did this activity together

50   **Writing for a purpose**

Postcard message

Do you know someone who lives a long way away?

● Write a postcard from where you live to them.

● Draw a picture of your home on the front of your card. Write your message on the back. If you do know someone who lives a long way away, put their address on, too.

impact WRITING HOMEWORK

Exciting foods

Do you have any food in your house from another country?

- Draw the food, and write down what it is, and where it comes from.

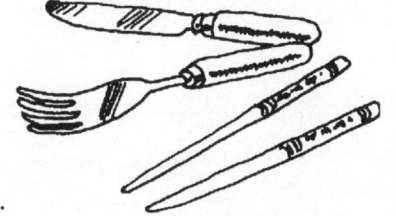

To the helper:

- Foods come from all over the world; if you look closely at any packaging you should find the country of origin.
- Talk about where the food comes from. Do you have an atlas at home? If so, see if you can find where it comes from. What kind of country is it? How similar is it to this country?

By having to find out, and then write down the country of origin of a certain food, the children are having to record useful information that we shall be using in the class for further written work.

_____ and
child

_____
helper(s)

_____
did this activity together

impact WRITING HOMEWORK

Writing for a purpose 51

To the helper:

- Have a look at any old birthday cards you might have at home for examples of birthday verses.
- The verse does not have to rhyme.

Writing verses in cards is one type of writing with a purpose. It encourages the children to concentrate on the special *style* of card verses. We shall be using the children's ideas for making cards at school.

_____ and

child

_____

helper(s)

did this activity together

Many happy returns

Imagine it's someone's birthday.

- Write a verse to go inside a birthday card.

52   **Writing for a purpose**

impact WRITING HOMEWORK

Merry Christmas!

- Write a verse to go inside a Christmas card.

To the helper:
- Have a look at any old Christmas cards you might have at home for examples of verses.
- The verse does not have to rhyme.

Writing verses in cards is one type of writing with a purpose. It encourages the children to concentrate on the special *style* of card verses. We shall be using the children's ideas for making cards at school.

_____and
child

_____
helper(s)

_____
did this activity together

impact WRITING HOMEWORK

Writing for a purpose 53

To the helper:

- Look out for a suitable picture. Talk about what is happening in the picture — are there other people there? What were you doing that day? Is it a funny picture?

Writing captions or labels for pictures involves a particular use of language. We shall discuss descriptive words, and different writing formats, for example speech bubbles in class.

_____and

child

_____

helper(s)

did this activity together

54   **Writing for a purpose**

This is your life!

Can you either find a photo of yourself, or draw a picture of yourself like a photo?

- Write a caption explaining your picture.

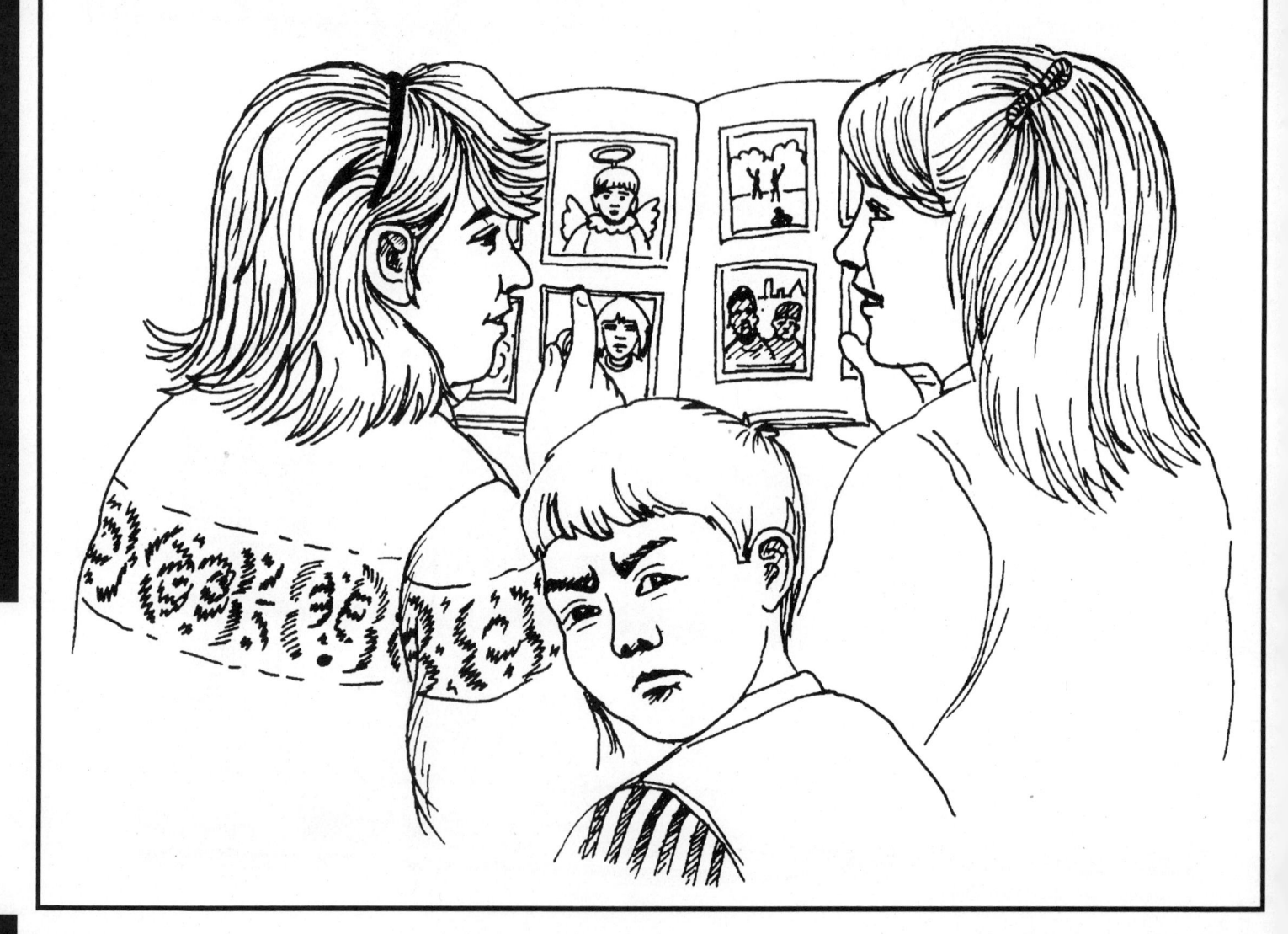

impact WRITING HOMEWORK

Musical words

What music do you like to listen to?

- Write down the name of your favourite song.

Do you know any of the words?

- Write down the words you know.

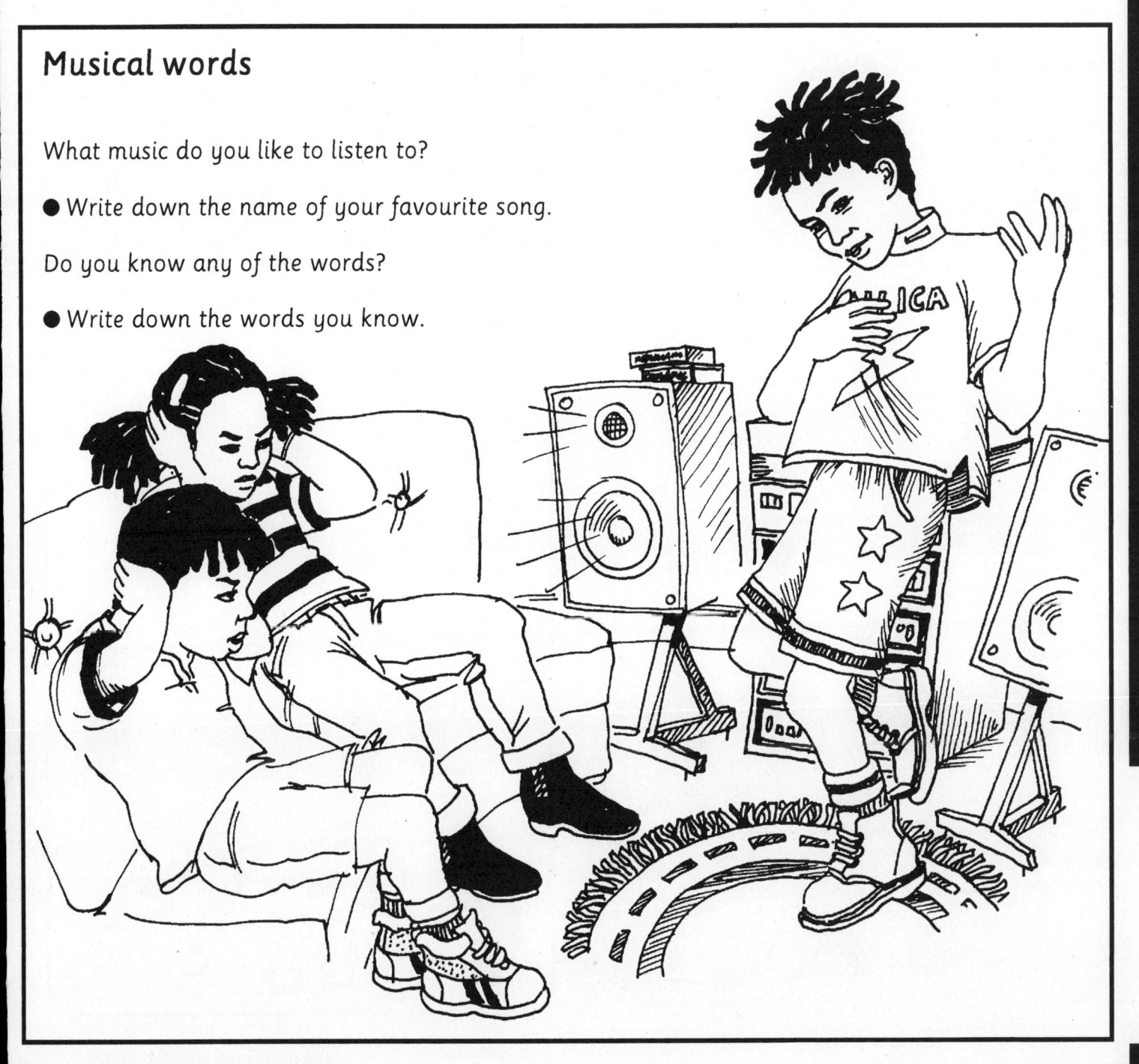

To the helper:
- Talk about the different sorts of music that you both like. Is there any kind that you agree on? What is your child's favourite song? Perhaps the words are written down somewhere on the sleeve, or in a book that you have. If so, try writing the words out from memory, and then check.
- Think about how words for songs are written out, generally they are written down like a poem.

Writing words for songs involves a particular use and style of language. We shall talk about the different songs and titles back at school.

_____ and
child

_____
helper(s)

_____
did this activity together

impact WRITING HOMEWORK

Writing for a purpose   55

To the helper:

- Talk about favourite types and pieces of music. Do you have an all-time favourite? What is it that you like about it? Does it conjure up a mood or a particular memory like a holiday? Do you have a favourite instrument or musician? Talk about these and how you will record this information.

Collecting and presenting information in various forms is an important skill in all areas of the curriculum. We shall be discussing the variety of musical taste and the ways of presenting this back at school.

_____and
child

_____
helper(s)

_____
did this activity together

56 **Writing for a purpose**

The sound of music

Ask some people at home what music they like.

- Ask them:
  - What is their favourite piece?
  - What is their favourite instrument?
  - Who is their favourite musician?

- Write down all this information.

impact WRITING HOMEWORK

Model instructions

Make a model of something.

You could use construction bricks or old boxes, etc.

● Write down the instructions for how to make your model for someone else to make it. Make sure that they know exactly what they will need to make it before they start.

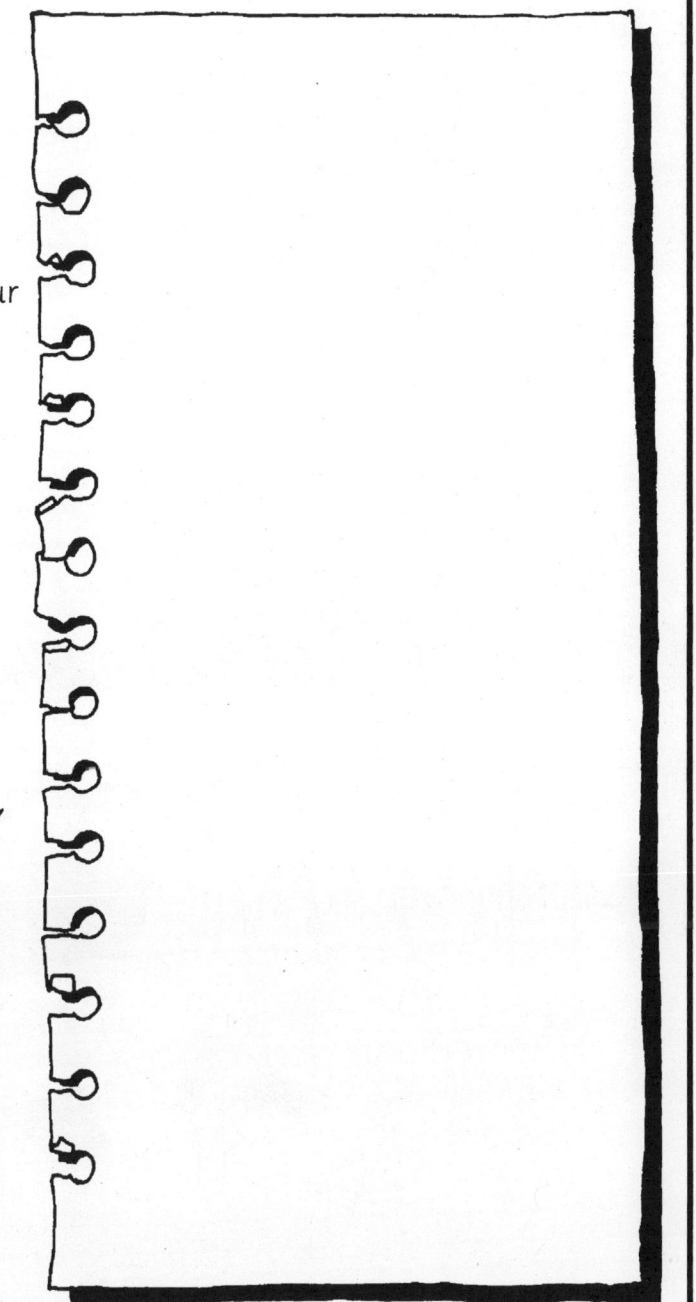

To the helper:

● Firstly, talk about the kind of model you want to make, what you will need, and how to remember how to make it in order to write it down. Will you be able to take the model apart again? Are you going to take notes of what you do as you go? Perhaps you could draw diagrams to make it clearer.

● You could work together to make the model.

Being able to write clear, concise instructions is an important skill in all areas of the curriculum. We shall attempt to make a few of the models at school using the children's instructions.

_____ and
child

_____
helper(s)

_____
did this activity together

impact WRITING HOMEWORK

Writing for a purpose 57

To the helper:

- Make a cup of tea with your child. Talk about all the things you will need. What things must you remember? What order do you do things in? Are you going to take notes of what you do as you go? Perhaps you could draw diagrams to make it clearer.

Being able to write clear, concise instructions is an important skill in all areas of the curriculum. We shall attempt to make a cup of tea at school using the children's instructions.

_____and
child

_____
helper(s)

_____
did this activity together

58   **Writing for a purpose**

Just my cup of tea

Do you know how to make a cup of tea?

- Watch someone at home, and then write out instructions for someone who does not know how to do it.

Don't forget to make a list of all the things they will need before they begin!

impact WRITING HOMEWORK

Looking for work!

● Write an advertisement for a notice board or shop window to advertise yourself.

You could be a 'dog walker' or a 'pet feeder' or a 'car washer'.

Think about what information needs to be in your advert.

Design it so that people will look at **your** advert first.

To the helper:
● Talk about the kind of information that needs to go in the advertisement. How much will you charge for the service, how will people contact you? How will you make it eye-catching?

Being able to present information in a clear and ordered way is an important skill. The posters that the children make will be displayed at school. We shall discuss the different methods the children have employed to catch people's attention, and investigate which styles are most effective.

_____and
child

_____
helper(s)

_____
did this activity together

impact WRITING HOMEWORK

Writing for a purpose

To the helper:

- Talk together about how easy it is to find various parts of the school. Is it difficult to find your child's classroom? How do parents know where to pick up their children each day? What about parents who do not read English?
- How will you set out the poster? Make sure it is clear and eye-catching!

Being able to present information in a clear and ordered way is an important skill. The posters will be displayed at school. We shall discuss the ways children caught people's attention, and investigate which styles are most effective.

_____ and
child

_____
helper(s)

did this activity together

60 **Writing for a purpose**

School signs

Talk with your helper about the school buildings. How easy is it to find your way around the school?

What information would be useful?

● Write down your ideas, and design a poster or sign that would help visitors to the school.

impact WRITING HOMEWORK

Road safety campaign

Have you seen the road safety poster which says 'Kill your speed'?

Can you think of another slogan that people will remember?

● Design a poster and write your slogan on it.

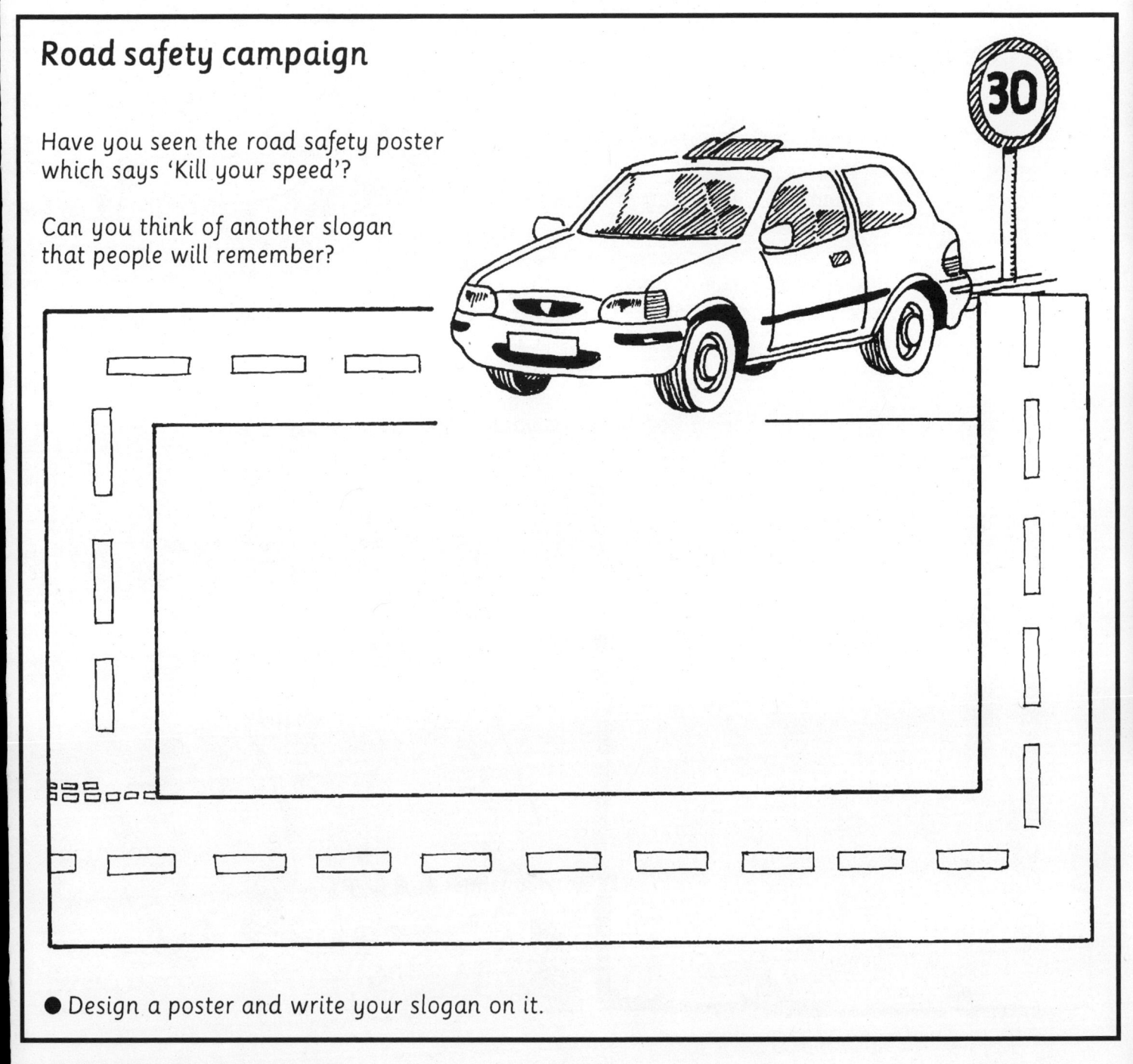

To the helper:
- Talk together about warnings you would like to give to motorists in your local area. Perhaps there is a particularly hazardous road near your home or school.
- How will you set out the poster? Make sure it is clear and eye-catching!

Being able to present information in a clear and ordered way is an important skill. The posters that the children make will be displayed at school. We shall discuss the different ways the children have caught people's attention, and investigate which styles are most effective.

_____and
child

_____
helper(s)

_____
did this activity together

impact WRITING HOMEWORK

Writing for a purpose 61

To the helper:

- Talk about the story; what has happened before, and what will happen next?
- Discuss the kind of information that needs to go in the message. Will you need to write much?

Writing clear, concise messages is an important purpose for writing. We shall be discussing the children's messages at school, and writing stories about their 'experiences'!

_____and
child

_____
helper(s)

did this activity together

Message in a bottle

Imagine that you are stranded on a desert island.

You are alone. There seems to be no way of letting anyone know where you are.

You have a pencil and a small piece of paper in your pocket. As you sit by the water, you spot a bottle floating by.

You decide to send someone a message in the bottle.

● Write down what your message will be, and tell your helper what happens next in the story.

62   Writing for a purpose

impact WRITING HOMEWORK

Magic beans

Imagine that you have just picked up a packet of magic beans.

- Write down the instructions that you might find on the packet.

To the helper:
- Talk about where you might find a packet of magic beans; did you buy them in a mysterious shop that disappeared the next day, were you sent the packet in the post, perhaps you swapped it at school for something?
- What kinds of unusual instructions might be on the packet? Perhaps you have to water it with strange ingredients. How long will it take to grow? **Being able to write clear, concise instructions is an important skill in all areas of the curriculum. We shall write full-length stories about the magic beans at school.**

_____ and
child

_____
helper(s)

_____
did this activity together

impact WRITING HOMEWORK

Writing for a purpose 63

To the helper:

- Talk about what instructions or directions you will need to add to your letters to make it clear and easy to follow. Show them some examples of letters, including 'business' letters, you have received recently. Write a letter to a relative or friend if you like using the format you have devised.

Being able to write clear concise instructions is an important skill in writing. Here we have used the *purpose* of writing instructions and applied it to the *form* of writing a letter (which is often difficult to learn for many children).

_____and
child

_____
helper(s)

_____
did this activity together

This is how you write a letter...

Write a letter to someone who doesn't know how to write a letter!

- Write instructions in the form of a letter to demonstrate how to do it. Use your letter as a model or template for them to learn from.

64 **Writing for a purpose**

impact WRITING HOMEWORK

Media slogan

Can you think of a slogan that you have seen in a magazine, or on the television?

- Write one down, the way it is in the advert.
- Now write down what you think it means.

To the helper:

- Have a look through a magazine, newspaper or a 'flyer' for ideas.
- Talk about the style of the writing and the colours used – do you think these are important?
- Talk about the messages a slogan gives you.

Looking closer at advertising slogans enables the children to question what they are told about a product. Advertising is potentially a very powerful use of language. We shall investigate the slogans the children find at school.

_____and
child

_____
helper(s)

_____
did this activity together

Writing for a purpose

To the helper:

- You can use a large piece of scrap paper like the reverse side of wallpaper if you have it to design your newspaper front page. Help with ideas for sketching out plans for the organisation of the page including the masthead (newspaper title), the banner (headline) and the columns. Leave space for an advert if your child wants to include one.

Learning to write in different styles is an important skill. This activity offers an opportunity to acquire 'journalese' and to think about the design and formatting features of newspaper front pages.

_____ and
child

_____
helper(s)

_____
did this activity together

Front page news

- Draw a picture of something funny, dramatic or exciting that has happened to you or your family.

- Write a caption to go underneath it.

- Write a short News Story to accompany the picture – think of a sub-title and organise it into columns like a newspaper.

- Write a banner headline to attract readers. Finally, don't forget to create a newspaper title (called a masthead).

66 Writing for a purpose

impact WRITING HOMEWORK

Atlas of my world

Can you draw a map of your street or immediate locality?

● Write in the names of places which are important to you such as where your friends live, your school, club, place of worship or adventure playground.

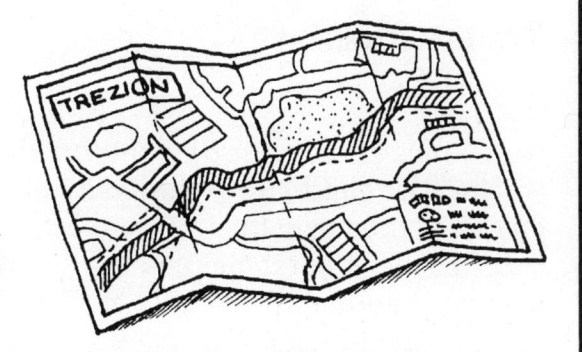

To the helper:

● Help your child draw up the list of local places they will include on the map. They may also need help with drawing to a rough scale, proportion, relative distances and with orientation of left and right etc.

Writing and drawing directions and maps is an important practical application of written language. It is a good example to show children that writing and drawing can fix complicated images and directions that are difficult to hold in your head.

_____and

child

_____

helper(s)

_____

did this activity together

impact WRITING HOMEWORK

Writing for a purpose 67

To the helper:

● Help your child list the points of argument and also discuss with them how to present them in order to be persuasive. Consider what the counter argument might be and how those points might be pre-empted.

Writing is an important medium for the ancient art of argument. Arguments are often more powerful when they have been edited, clarified and honed by the process of writing.

_____ and

child

_____

helper(s)

did this activity together

Please Miss!

Sometimes on the last day of term teachers let children take in their favourite toys to school. Persuade your teacher that some of your toys have **so** much educational value that you should be allowed to bring them in more often!

● Write four points of argument to convince your teacher.

Writing for a purpose

impact WRITING HOMEWORK

Send out for pizza!

- Write a leaflet for a 'Pizza by phone' delivery company. Make it colourful and appealing. What special offers will you have on it to attract custom?

To the helper:

- Have a look at some of the junk mail adverts and leaflets you get through the door, especially those for food outlets like pizzas or other ethnic food delivery or take aways. Talk about what techniques are used to attract custom, such as colour schemes, block lettering or special offers.
- Help with design features and difficult spellings.

The language of advertising is a powerful medium. Writing adverts and looking critically at advertising strategies gives children an opportunity to question methods used.

_____and
child

_____
helper(s)

did this activity together

impact WRITING HOMEWORK

Writing for a purpose 69

To the helper:

- Talk together about how music helps people use their imagination and how it can influence mood. Write a list of song titles, music and musicians which have done this for you. Introduce them to your child if they have never heard them. Send this list in to school for the class collection if you like!

Collecting information and presenting it in various forms is an important skill in all areas of the curriculum. In school we shall be discussing the variety of musical taste and the ways of presenting this information.

_____and

child

_____

helper(s)

_____

did this activity together

70 Writing for a purpose

The image of music

Can music make pictures? Has a particular piece of music ever given you an image of something?

- Write down the names of pieces of music, song titles or musicians whose music is associated with evoking particular images.

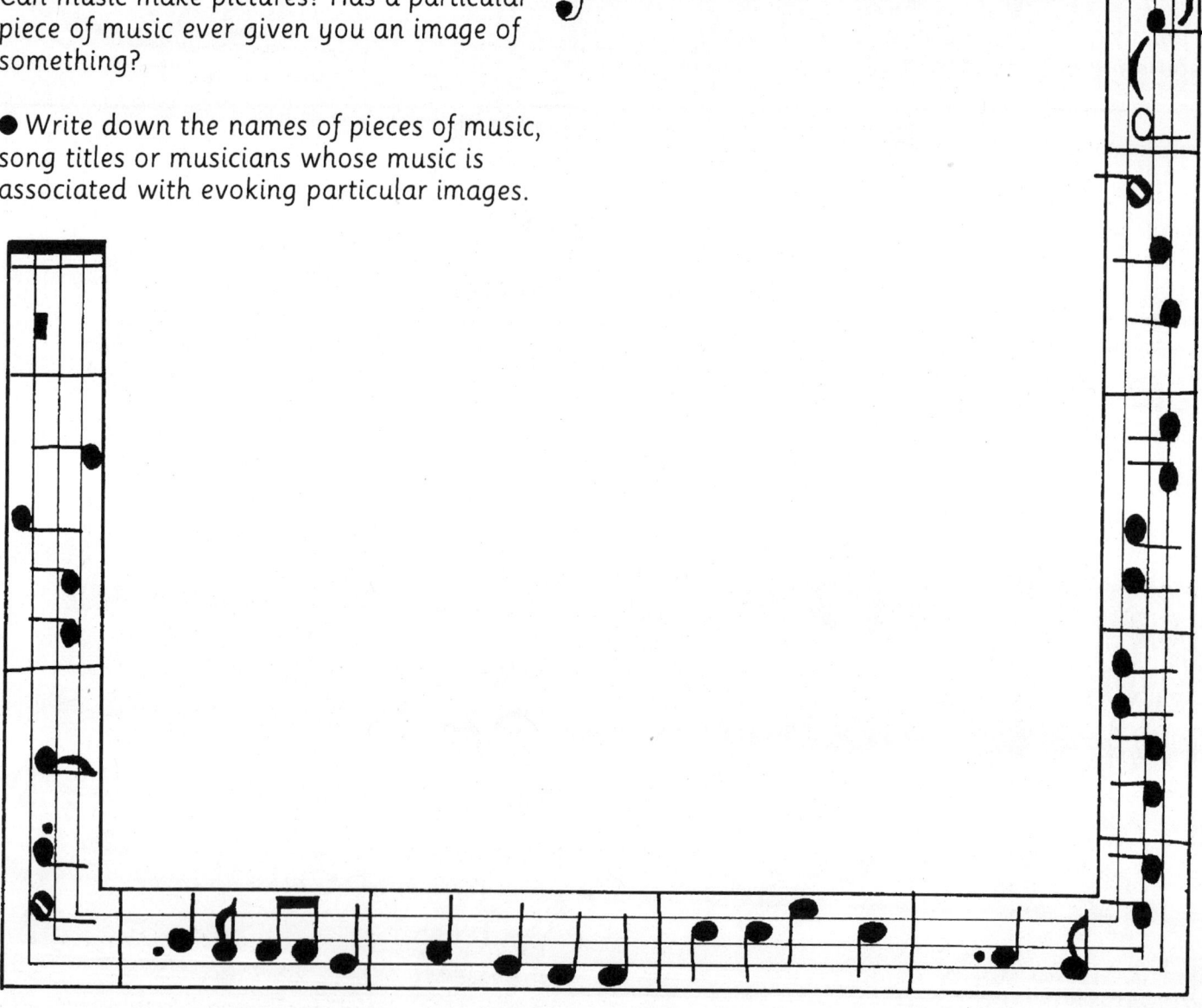

impact WRITING HOMEWORK

Teachers' Notes
YEAR FIVE

Weather forecasting It will be useful to have as many of these forecasts back in the classroom before the weather for next week really starts! So encourage the children to bring this one back promptly. When the forecasts come back, talk about the range of conditions the children have forecast for your area. On what have they based their predictions? Have they used information from the television, or newspaper? When the children read out their reports, are they in the *style* of a weather forecast? Which children were most accurate in their weather forecasts?

Playground rhymes Talk about the rhymes that the children bring in. Can they sing or say any of them without the words written down? Try to teach them to the rest of the class. Invite in someone from the local community who was at school a long time ago to teach the children some rhymes and games. Compile all the rhymes into a class book.

Pen-friend Discuss how the children have described their area. What sort of descriptive words have they used? Make a list of the words and phrases they have chosen. Divide these and categorise them under the headings 'positive' and 'negative'. For example, 'noisy' might be under negative whereas 'lively' might be under positive. How well do the children know their area?

This is me Read out some of the children's descriptions – can the other children guess who they are? Now ask them to write a short paragraph which describes themselves in such a way that no-one would guess it was them! They can only say true things – but perhaps give information which is misleading or not so well known! For example, 'Born at midnight in the middle of winter, in a cold farmhouse...'.

Captions Display the children's pictures, and their captions, so that the other children can read them too. Have the children managed to make their captions funny? How are they funny? Talk about the different ways there are to caption a picture; for example, with a new title, or speech bubble. Perhaps you could start a caption competition. Look out for an amusing or odd picture, and pin it up on the wall. The children can then write suitable funny captions to go with the picture. They could pin up their caption next to the picture with their name on it.

Breakfast instructions Ask one of the children to read out their instructions. Have they tested them out at home? Now try to imagine that a blind child is coming to join your class; she is going to have packed lunches. Write down instructions for her to come from the classroom, to fetch her lunchbox, and then to sit at the table where she would normally eat. What special things will you need to consider if she cannot see? (You will have to imagine also that these instructions will be read out to her.) Test out some of the sets of instructions on children wearing blindfolds.

It makes me so angry!/It's just not good enough! When the children bring back their letters, talk about how different the letter might have been if they were complaining about a similar thing to a grandparent or neighbour. Show them that it does make a difference who the letter is for, and what the letter is about, in the way the letter is structured and phrased.

'I say, I say, I say...' Jokes often use puns, or puns of parts of words to make them funny. Look at a few of the children's jokes, and take them apart – what is it that makes this joke funny? Put all the children's jokes into a class book of jokes that the children can illustrate. Talk about other kinds of puns; can the children think of any more?

Healthy lunchbox How healthy are the school dinners or lunchboxes eaten at your school? Investigate the range of foods available, and what is actually eaten. What about children who are vegetarian; is there an attractive option for them? Can you find any 'recommendations' or directives that outline what a good school dinner should be? Does your school match up to it? What could you do about it if not?

Sweet or savoury? Make a class list of all the foods the children have on their lists. Categorise the foods under different headings: sweet/sour, fruit, cakes, biscuits, vegetables, meat, cereal etc. Make a class-graph of all the different types of food.

Can you cook? When the children bring back their recipes into class, look at the range of ingredients required, and buy enough to make a few of the examples. Put the children in groups to follow the recipes; directly following the instructions. What do they come up with? Are they edible? Now cut the foods up into tiny, bite-size pieces. Let everyone have a taste. Will anyone be brave enough to try a food they have never tried before? Devise a questionnaire with the children rating the foods on presentation, texture, taste and originality.

Remember! Remember! Buy some pads of removable self-adhesive notes and encourage the children to write reminder notes to each other. They can stick them on doors and windows, books and bags. Discuss other memory aids such as anagrams and mnemonic phrases and make a collection of them for a display.

Spend! Spend! Spend! Offer children other exercises in ordering their personal priorities such as 'Ten life ambitions to fulfil' or 'Five resolutions for this year'. Other ordered lists might be to draw up 'Five rules for good behaviour in class' or 'Dos and Don'ts in the playground' or 'The five good things about my mum'.

Carnivore or herbivore? Children can write fact sheets or information booklets about the pros and cons of meat eating and vegetarianism. Organise debates for children to write speeches to present their arguments. Posters, leaflets, handbills, manifestos can all be designed and written to present the case for and against.

This is your life! Set the children a series of exercises on writing to persuade, using the distinctions of reason (using logic, evidence or cause and effect conclusions), character (referring to reputable and trusted others) and emotion (appeals others are likely to empathise with on the basis of self-interest) to categorise and clarify their arguments. Topics could include school organisational issues like extending the duration of playtimes or reducing the frequency of homework. Organise opportunities for debating and public speaking. Write posters, handbills, manifestos. Discuss distinctions between persuasion and propaganda; between persuasive arguments and advertisements.

Pros and cons Listing pros and cons could become a regular feature of decision-making in the classroom. Set the children some difficult questions and dilemmas such as 'Giving up sweets' or 'Saving my pocket money'.

Keep it simple! Collect examples of advertising slogans on posters and the pages of magazines and newspapers. Examine and discuss the meanings of the slogans in relation to the intended audiences. Do they use loaded phrases or deceptive language? Discuss the distinctions between persuasion and propaganda. Compare advertising slogans and political slogans. Write your own versions.

Save the whale Look at the way propaganda is used by pressure groups and charities. Send for material by organisations like Greenpeace, Amnesty International and Oxfam. Compare this material to other forms of propaganda like that used during the Second World War by the Ministry of Defence. Compare distinctions of propaganda to advertising. Make a list of loaded words (best buy, discounted, extra strong, longer lasting) and euphemisms used in wars (friendly fire, neutralise, pin-point bombing). Greenpeace, Canonbury Villas, London N1 2PN; Amnesty International, British Section, 99-119 Rosebury Avenue, London EC1R 4RE; Oxfam, 274 Banbury Road, Oxford OX2 7DZ

Believe it or not Make some cards with facts and opinions written on them and set groups of children discussion tasks. Set them tasks of writing statements of fact and opinion which challenge each other.

I can icon Make collections of icons, symbols and signs used for administrative, commercial, legal and institutional purposes. Set the children tasks of writing iconographic instructions for operating classroom utilities like computer software. Write some narratives using similar symbols (also available on most word-processing packages as alternative font styles). Can others 'read' it? Look at Egyptian hieroglyphics.

Thank you for nothing! This activity develops the concept of persuasion. Set the children tasks of letter writing that demands them to be diplomatic in difficult social situations like declining invitations, gifts and offers of favours. Discuss and list words and phrases that express appreciation and others that express polite but direct refusal. Role play them. Compare the use of written and oral language in similar settings.

Watch this space Make a class diary with swimming and music lessons, library and museum visits, PE and games sessions and outings in. Children could make personal diaries of times, events and appointments in the school timetable. Surveys about TV-watching habits could be compiled from the diaries brought back to school.

Step by step/Cause and effect Make cards with a variety of causes and effects for children to discuss and organise in logical steps. Environmental and social issues (like climate change, traffic congestion, bullying, litter, drug and alcohol abuse) could be used. Experiment with a variety of graphic methods for showing cause and effect, using flow charts, circular diagrams, steps or panels.

Address book Discuss the children's address books. Are there any names which are in more than one person's book? Discuss which order you would write the names if you have more than one name under one letter. For example, 'Banks' comes before 'Brown'. Make a class address book for all the children in the class. They can draw a picture of themselves to go with their entry – and perhaps write a short biography.

72 **Writing for a purpose**

impact WRITING HOMEWORK

Weather forecasting

- Write a weather forecast for next week.

You could watch the television, listen to the radio or look in a newspaper to help you find out what sorts of weather you might forecast.

To the helper:
- Talk about the kind of information you are given in a weather forecast. How much detail are you given, does it vary from source to source? Why do people want to know what the weather is going to be like in advance?
- Talk about how the information is presented; do they use maps or charts to help explain the forecast?

Writing a weather forecast is a specific style of writing for a purpose. The writing needs to be clear and concise. We shall compare forecasts at school, and see who was the most accurate.

_____and

child

_____

helper(s)

_____

did this activity together

impact WRITING HOMEWORK

Writing for a purpose 73

To the helper:

- Talk about the rhymes that you used to sing at school. Can you remember any clapping, skipping or chanting songs?
- Can you ask someone that was at school a very long time ago for their memories?

Recording information is a particularly important and useful skill in all areas of the curriculum. We shall look at the songs and rhymes at school, and see if we know any of them – have any disappeared or changed over time?

_____ and
child

_____
helper(s)

did this activity together

Playground rhymes

'A sailor went to sea, sea, sea
To see what he could see, see, see...'

This is an old playground song that you still hear sometimes.

- Talk to someone who does not go to school any more and see if they can remember any other playground songs.
- Write them down.

74 **Writing for a purpose**

impact WRITING HOMEWORK

Pen-friend

Imagine you are writing a letter to someone for the first time.

How would you describe the place where you live?

- Write down your description.

To the helper:

- Talk about the place where you live. What are the main features: is it a town, city, village or farm? How does where you live affect the way you live, for example do you need a car or can you walk to school? Do friends live nearby; do you use a lift to get to your flat etc? What do you think about the place where you live; would you recommend it to someone else?

Describing what you know well to someone who has never seen it before requires you to see it through someone else's eyes. This encourages the use of precise language.

_____and
child

_____
helper(s)

did this activity together

impact WRITING HOMEWORK

Writing for a purpose

To the helper:

- Talk to your child about themselves. What do they look like? What do they like to wear? Are they quiet, lively or serious? What kinds of sport, music, hobbies do they like? Can you think of anything else which might be interesting to someone who has never met your child?

Describing yourself to someone who has never seen or met you before requires you to see yourself through someone else's eyes. This encourages the use of precise language.

_____and
child

_____
helper(s)

_____
did this activity together

This is me

Write a portrait of yourself to a distant relative who you have never met!

How would you describe yourself?

● Write down your description.

DESCRIPTION
I am ten years old, tall with brown hair and glasses. I am brilliant at all sports, extremely good looking and amazingly modest.

76   Writing for a purpose

impact WRITING HOMEWORK

Captions

Find an interesting image from a magazine, and cut it out. If there is any writing on it cover it up, or cut that off, too.

- Design a new caption to go with your image that changes the meaning of the picture.

To the helper:

- Look through any newspapers or magazines you have at home for inspiration. Can you find one that you could give a funny caption?

Writing captions or labels for pictures involves a particular use of language. We shall discuss descriptive words, and different writing formats, for example speech bubbles in class.

_____ and
child

_____
helper(s)

_____
did this activity together

impact WRITING HOMEWORK

Writing for a purpose

To the helper:

- This task will require a lot of thinking time and some time for testing out.
- You may need to help with some of the writing, and the 'testing'!

This activity will make the children think very carefully about what they write, and how they write it. Back in the classroom we shall examine some of these instructions to see if they are clear and easy to understand.

_____ and
child

_____
helper(s)

_____
did this activity together

78   **Writing for a purpose**

Breakfast instructions

Imagine that a friend has come to stay who has never seen your kitchen before.

● Write out instructions so that they can find all they would need for a good breakfast.

Think about what they will need to know:
- Where is the milk?
- Where are the plates, cups, knives etc.?
- Where is the rubbish bin?

Perhaps you could draw them a plan to help!

● Get someone to try out your instructions pretending that they don't know your kitchen.

impact WRITING HOMEWORK

It makes me so angry!

What makes you really mad? What do people do that really annoys you?

- Write a letter to the newspaper letting off steam about it!

To the helper:
- Talk about the things that people write to the newspaper about. Perhaps you have a newspaper at home that you can refer to.
- Talk about how you would set out a letter to the paper; who would you address it to, and would you sign your real name, or a 'pen name' such as 'Angry of Amersham'?

Writing a letter to the newspaper complaining about something requires an awareness of certain conventions within writing. The skills used in writing a clear letter are very important, and will be useful to the children in the future.

_____ and
child

_____
helper(s)

_____
did this activity together

impact WRITING HOMEWORK

Writing for a purpose 79

To the helper:

- Talk about the kind of thing that your child could say about the toy; how much they had looked forward to buying it, how disappointed they were when it broke etc.
- Talk about how you would set out a letter to the manufacturers and who you would address it to.

Writing a letter to a company complaining about something requires the children to be aware of certain writing conventions. The skills used in writing a clear letter are very important, and will be useful to the children in the future.

_____ and
child

_____
helper(s)

did this activity together

80 Writing for a purpose

It's just not good enough!

Imagine that a very expensive toy that you bought with your birthday money has broken, just two days after you bought it.

● Write a letter of complaint to the manufacturers explaining why you are angry.

impact WRITING HOMEWORK

'I say, I say, I say...'

Do you know any 'I say, I say, I say...' jokes?

● Write down three of them.

Ask your helper if they know any if you get stuck.

To the helper:

● Talk about the jokes your child comes home with from school; are there any that really made you laugh?
● Talk about how you will write down the jokes; how will you show how to *say* the jokes?

Back at school, we shall tell one another the jokes, and discuss what makes them funny. We shall look closer at puns, and the way the English language can at one time be confusing, and at others funny!

_____ and
child

_____
helper(s)

_____
did this activity together

impact WRITING HOMEWORK

Writing for a purpose 81

To the helper:

● Talk about the lunches they have at school now. How healthy are they? How could you improve on them?

Writing lists is an important skill which will be useful to the children in several areas of their life in the future. We shall discuss the list of healthy foods that the children thought of in the class.

_____ and
child

_____
helper(s)

did this activity together

82 **Writing for a purpose**

Healthy lunchbox

If you were going to pack your own lunch, what healthy things could you put in it? Would you eat those things?

● Write down five healthy items for a lunchbox that you **would** eat.

impact WRITING HOMEWORK

Sweet or savoury?

Does anyone in your family have a sweet tooth?

Ask some friends and family and find out what their favourite foods are. Are they sweet or savoury?

- Write them down.

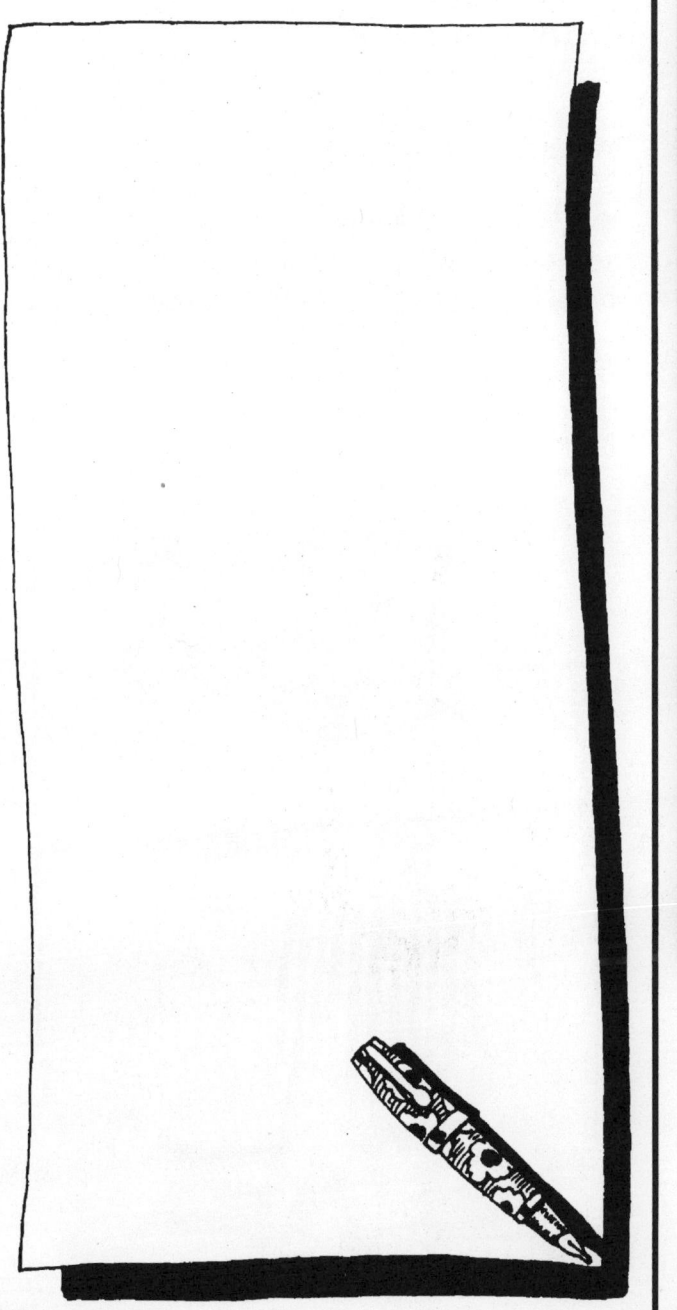

To the helper:

- Talk about the difference between sweet and savoury. Is there any other kind of flavour?

Writing lists is an important skill which will be useful to the children in several areas of their life in the future. We shall discuss the taste preferences that the children found out about in the class.

_____ and
child

_____
helper(s)

_____
did this activity together

impact WRITING HOMEWORK

Writing for a purpose 83

To the helper:

- Does your child ever cook at home? Look together in a recipe book or magazine for ideas on how to set out the information.
- Choose something simple.

Writing a recipe is one example of writing instructions. They need to be clear and structured for someone else to follow them. We shall try a few of the recipes at school.

_____ and
child

_____
helper(s)

_____
did this activity together

Can you cook?

Are you a good cook?

● Write out the instructions to make something which you have made before (either at school or at home).

Don't forget that you will need to describe the ingredients needed, and the method.

TODAY'S MENU

84 **Writing for a purpose**

impact WRITING HOMEWORK

Remember! Remember!

- Write yourself a reminder note to remember to do something which you often forget. It might be:
- 'Remember to put out the rubbish bag this week!' or
- 'Remember to water the plants' or even
- 'Remember to remind dad about helping me do my IMPACT!'

To the helper:

- Discuss what your child often forgets or needs to remember, for example to take their PE kit to school each Tuesday.
- Make a list of all the things they need to remember.

Writing is an important aid to memory and this activity helps children realise the potential of using writing for this function.

_____and

child

_____

helper(s)

_____

did this activity together

impact WRITING HOMEWORK

Writing for a purpose 85

To the helper:

- Have some fun making a list of the things you and your family would like to buy. Remember, you have a limited amount so make sure you include (approximate) costings to your list of items.
- Discuss ways of listing your items, either by order of importance, value or some other criteria.

Writing a list of items by specific criteria helps give order to our thoughts and helps us to reflect on priorities.

_____and
child

_____
helper(s)

_____
did this activity together

86 **Writing for a purpose**

Spend! Spend! Spend!

Imagine that you have been given a million pounds to spend!

● Make a list of what you will do with the money, and put your ideas in order – the one you **most** want first!

impact WRITING HOMEWORK

Carnivore or herbivore?

Some people eat meat (carnivores) and some are vegetarians (herbivores). What are you?

- Give two reasons why you are what you are. Discuss these with your helper. Would anything change your mind?

To the helper:

- Discuss the pros and cons of meat eating and vegetarianism. Help your child write down some of these ideas and select the two most convincing and persuasive points to express their personal point of view. If there is something about someone else's point of view that they can see, write a line about that at the end.

Writing can be an important vehicle for clarifying thoughts about points of argument and reflecting on counter points and alternative views.

_____ and
child

_____
helper(s)

did this activity together

impact WRITING HOMEWORK

Writing for a purpose 87

To the helper:

- Help your child think of three different persuasive points: one based on *reason* ('professional footballers earn a lot of money'); one based on *character* ('Gary Lineker was a footballer') and one based on *emotion* ('I want to score goals at a Cup Final!').
- Think of a way of presenting the argument persuasively, such as using drawings, speech bubbles or spider-grams.

Using writing to persuade is an important skill because through writing, people often contemplate and consider argument more carefully.

_____ and
child

_____
helper(s)

_____
did this activity together

88   **Writing for a purpose**

This is your life!

What will you be when you're an adult?

- Write down three points that you would use to persuade your mum or dad that becoming one of these would be a good idea:
  - professional footballer
  - supermodel
  - film star
  - pop star
  - astronaut.

Or think of your own idea.

impact WRITING HOMEWORK

Pros and cons

Sometimes it's hard to make a decision about a difficult subject. Writing a list of pros and cons can help.

Think of a difficult personal question or decision.

● Write out the pros in one column and the cons in another.

Pros	Cons

To the helper:

● Discuss some difficult dilemmas that might benefit from this approach. Discuss the pros and cons of the question as your child writes them down.

Writing to help us think and reflect is an important function of written language.

_____ and
child

_____
helper(s)

_____
did this activity together

impact WRITING HOMEWORK

Writing for a purpose   89

To the helper:

- Make a list of advertising slogans and mottos from the TV, newspapers and magazines. Discuss why many are short and simple but have a direct impact.
- Think of a product and make up some punchy advertising slogans that you think will capture the imagination of potential consumers.

Advertising slogans are a powerful form of persuasive writing designed to appeal to our reason and emotions. Learning to write such slogans will help us understand how that power works.

_____ and
child

_____
helper(s)

_____

did this activity together

Keep it simple!

Advertisers often use short phrases (especially when selling their products to young people).

- Think of some examples.
- Make a list.
- Now make up one for your favourite product.

BUY THE BEST YOU DESERVE IT!

90 **Writing for a purpose**

impact WRITING HOMEWORK

Save the whale

Is there an issue which you really care about?

- Design a T-shirt with a logo that expresses your concern for the issue.
- Draw it and design the lettering, logo and graphics to go on it.

To the helper:

- Talk about some issues that concern you and your child. Suggest some slogans that express concern for the issue.
- Try to appeal to people's emotions in your choice of words. Think of some other design features like a logo or an image that will add to the power of the message.

Writing is used for propaganda purposes. It uses emotive images and language to win support for urgent issues.

_____ and
child

_____
helper(s)

_____
did this activity together

Writing for a purpose

impact WRITING HOMEWORK

To the helper:

- Sort out the statements and write the appropriate letter in each box.
- Encourage your child to add other comments which might explain the statements.

Writing is an aid in discussing propositions, facts and opinions because the statements are written down, observable and can be referred to directly, whereas oral statements are often misconstrued, contested and argued over.

_____ and
child

_____
helper(s)

_____
did this activity together

Believe it or not

When discussing a point of argument people use facts and opinions to try to persuade. Facts are statements which are known to be true. Opinions are personal beliefs.

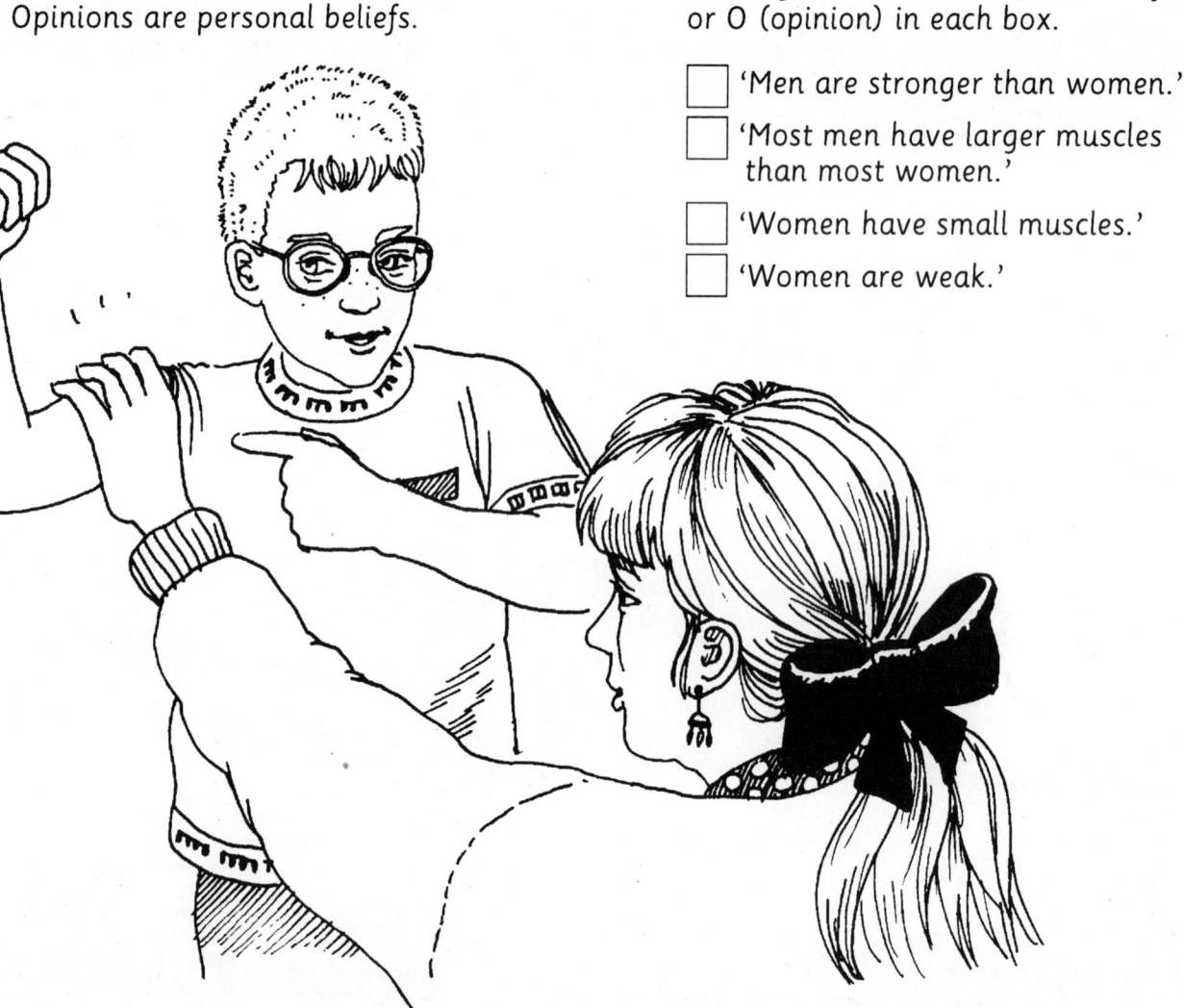

● Talk to your helper about which of these are facts and which are opinions. When you have decided, write F (fact) or O (opinion) in each box.

☐ 'Men are stronger than women.'

☐ 'Most men have larger muscles than most women.'

☐ 'Women have small muscles.'

☐ 'Women are weak.'

Writing for a purpose

impact WRITING HOMEWORK

I can icon

You see icons like these on video recorders, CD and tape players. They are used as a way of explaining instructions to people without relying on words.

● Can you write a set of instructions to help someone set the video to record a favourite programme using icons and symbols? (Use as few words as possible.)

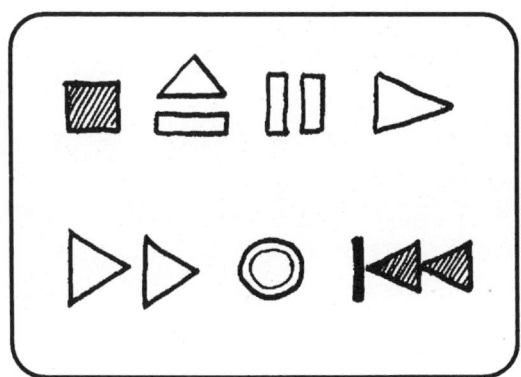

To the helper:

● This is a bit like Egyptian hieroglyphics! Remember that instructions need to be clear and easy to follow so use symbols like a finger (to press) and a clock face (for setting time). Try it out on someone to see if your instructions can be followed!

Writing pictorial or ideographic symbols can be a more effective form of communication than alphabetic symbols because a whole idea is expressed which doesn't need to be decoded into sound.

_____ and
child

_____
helper(s)

_____
did this activity together

Writing for a purpose

To the helper:

● Help your child choose the right words in order to write a letter which is appreciative, tactful and polite. Make a list of appropriate words and phrases.

Writing offers the opportunity to couch words and phrases that would be difficult to say in a personal face-to-face situation. This activity demands writing for more than one purpose.

_____and
child

_____
helper(s)

_____

did this activity together

Writing for a purpose

Thank you for nothing!

Have you ever received a present that you didn't want?

● Write a 'thank you letter' to someone who gave you such a present. Don't tell any lies, but you must write in such a way that you don't hurt their feelings.

Watch this space

- Make a TV diary of all your favourite programmes so that you won't forget to watch or videotape them.

- Arrange the programmes by days of the week and times of the day. Make a book by folding some paper and stapling or sewing the edge.

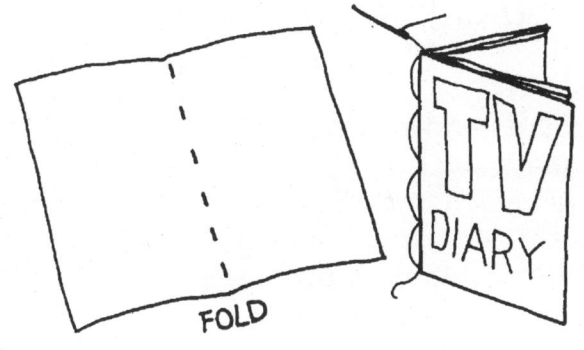

To the helper:

- Make suggestions about organising the diary so that it is easy to read and refer to. For example, different channels could be colour coded in columns and programmes could be sectioned in rows.

One of the main functions of writing is to organise time and information.

_____and
child

_____
helper(s)

_____
did this activity together

impact WRITING HOMEWORK

Writing for a purpose 95

To the helper:

- Think of a suitable issue such as environmental damage, wildlife destruction or homelessness and discuss the possible causes. List them. Does one cause another? Organise them in steps.

Showing causes and effects in steps is a technique of writing to help us think logically.

_____ and

child

_____

helper(s)

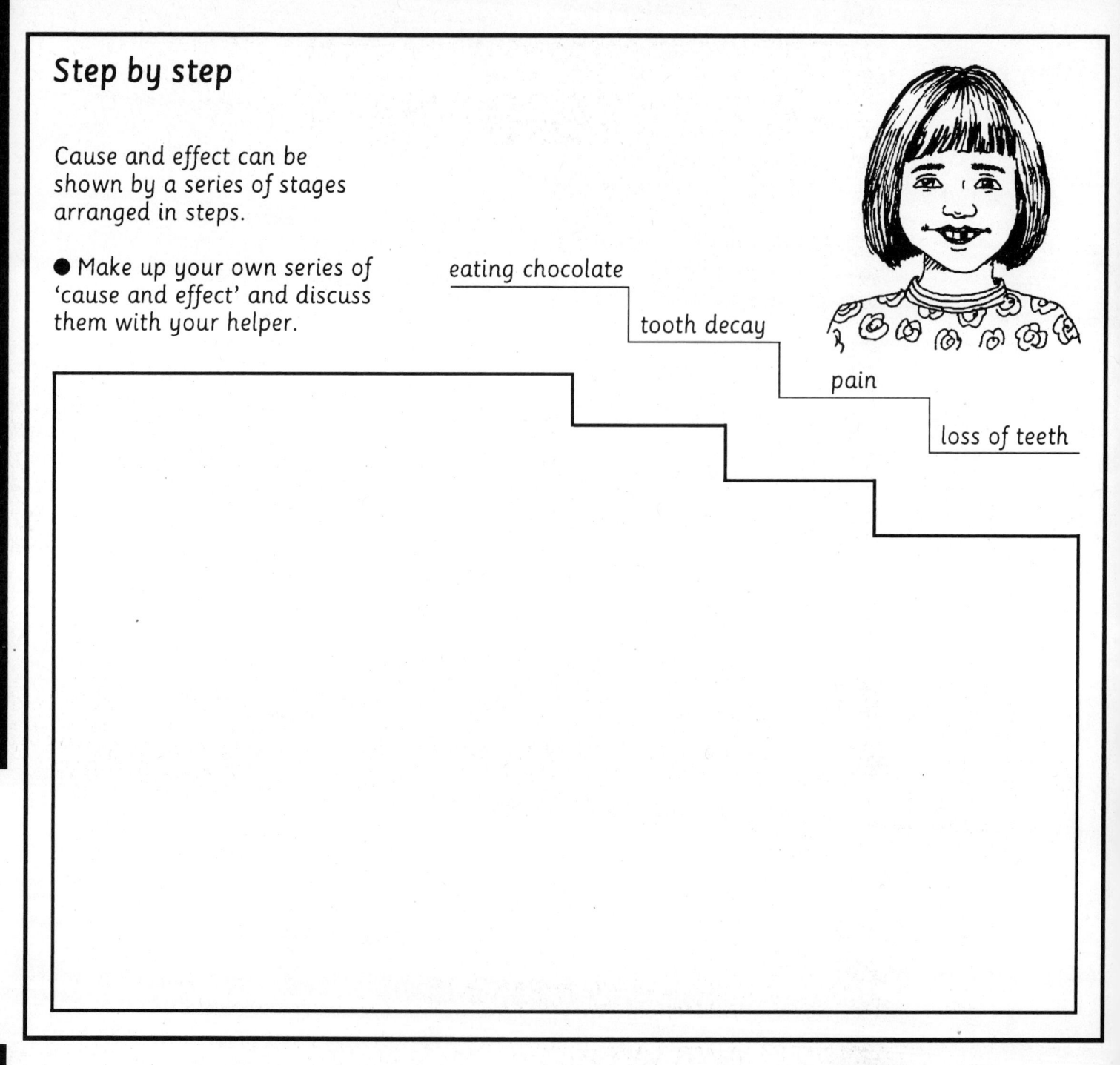

did this activity together

Writing for a purpose

Step by step

Cause and effect can be shown by a series of stages arranged in steps.

- Make up your own series of 'cause and effect' and discuss them with your helper.

eating chocolate

tooth decay

pain

loss of teeth

impact WRITING HOMEWORK

Cause and effect

Look at this list of words and phrases. Talk to your helper about which ones might be the cause and which ones the effect, for example does **smoking cause lung cancer** or does **lung cancer cause smoking**? Write a list of all the possible causes and effects.

smoking
lung cancer
bad breath
eating fatty foods
heart disease
stress

To the helper:
- Write out the phrases on separate pieces of paper and shuffle various combinations to discuss which are causes and which are effects. Your child may want to add some comments about whether they are all definitely causes.

Written language provides the possibility of making thought processes visible and helps to develop and organise ideas.

_____ and
child

_____
helper(s)

did this activity together

impact WRITING HOMEWORK

Writing for a purpose 97

To the helper:

- Help your child find as many addresses as they can.
- Talk about how you sort things into alphabetical order. What about people whose names start with the same letter?

Compiling an address list requires the children to use alphabetical and organising skills for a useful purpose.

_____ and
child

_____
helper(s)

_____
did this activity together

Address book

- Collect your friends' and relatives' addresses.
- Sort them into alphabetical order and write them out like an address book.

98 **Writing for a purpose**

impact WRITING HOMEWORK

Teachers' Notes
YEAR SIX

TV survey Use the information to compile a daily chart of viewing habits. What type of programmes have been chosen? Sport, drama, current affairs, soap, animation, etc? Perhaps you could write your own soap in class; develop a setting, character descriptions, and the beginnings of a plot. The children could work in groups each week to work collaboratively.

Personal advertisement Collect the children's descriptions, and read out a few of them. How many words did you have to read out before the children guessed who it was? Would the child's friends agree that their description is accurate? If friends were to write descriptions of one another, would they say the same things as the children have written about themselves? What if you (the teacher) were to write descriptions of the children; how similar would they be?

Wanted! Read out some of the children's descriptions. Is there anyone in the class who would fit the description? Did the children have anyone in mind when they wrote it? Think of situations when you might need a companion; perhaps for a holiday, or to share your hobby with you.

Stop the press! Get the children to read out their newspaper reports. Are the stories recognisable form the books they are reading? What points have they focused on? Who are they aiming the report at? What is it about this style of writing that makes it sound like a newspaper report? If you have a newspaper programme on your computer, make up a newspaper from the articles.

Saga in fifty words Set the children a variety of themes for writing 'fifty word sagas'. Model and exemplify the re-drafting and editing process involved. Model a variety of beginnings and endings that leave the children to fill in the gaps.

Calling Iceland Pin up a map of Europe, mark on the time zones, and talk to the children about what time it would be in countries other than Iceland. Group the children and ask them to find out what codes are needed to dial to ring some other European countries. Extend the work by using the codes as the basis for a piece of creative writing – perhaps a 'phone conversation' which takes place from here to Iceland (or another country in Europe).

Phone book Working in small groups or pairs, the children could look up one of their friends, or a local business number. The children can then do a piece of creative writing based on taking a name and phone number from the phone book and 'creating' a character. They can describe what this (fictitious) person does, what family they have and invent a short biography!

Magazine freebies Talk about the offers that the children had to send off for; what information did they require? What kind of things can you get for free? Talk about the different forms of letter that people need to write and how they differ from one another. For example, a bill or invoice, a letter of complaint, a congratulations letter, a get well letter, a letter of condolence, a job application, or a letter to a best friend.

Note-taker Taking notes is a skill that really needs to be taught. When the children bring back their notes, discuss what were the important things to remember: not writing everything out but using key words, using shorthand or diagrams. Practise taking notes from other television programmes, or if you have a visiting speaker in school.

Long time no see This is quite a difficult task for a lot of children; it requires them to stand back and look at themselves, and see how they have changed over the years. When the children bring back their letters into class, discuss with them what they considered to be the most difficult part. Talk about how it can be quite difficult to 'address' a letter, without being familiar with the person they are writing to. How did they solve this problem? Did they imagine that they were writing to a good friend, and so use a written monologue form, or did they choose to be more formal?

Improving your environment! This demands several skills. The children need to be clear about their proposal, and be able to 'sell' the idea; their thoughts will have to be organised (suggest that they number their points, or write under headed paragraphs); and they will need to have some idea of who they are sending their letter to. Display the children's proposals and pick out the good points. Perhaps someone has headed their letter with a title, perhaps someone else has numbered their points, and kept the detail to a minimum.

Home rules Ask the children to write up their rules on a large sheet of paper so everyone can read them. Display them so that the children can talk about them. Are there any they would like to change or remove once they have thought about them? Are there any that occur frequently on all of the sheets of rules? Are the rules largely 'do' rules or 'don't' rules? Get the children to rephrase their rules into all positive rules.

There should be a law against it! Talk to the children about the kind of thing they might want to criminalise; a few examples are given in the note to the helper. Talk about how you would write down a new law; how might you phrase it so that there were no loopholes? Ask the children to explain their ideas and answer 'What if...?' questions from the other children. Has anyone thought of a very sensible law? Write to an MP outlining your most sensible

impact WRITING HOMEWORK

Writing for a purpose 99

law, explaining why you think it is so sensible. Ask the children to write speeches and take part in a 'parliamentary debate' to discuss all their ideas.

Legalise it! Children could debate controversial issues: speed limits, the age of consent for driving/drug use/smoking/sex/gambling (arcades and the Lottery).

Sporty points How many different sports did the children cover? Can they think of any sports which were missed out? Perhaps you can write some class lists of points for some of the sports which were missed? Look at several sets of instructions for the same sport. Were they all identical? Did some people take a different view about what it was important to remember? Paint large pictures of people doing the different sports. Word-process the lists of instructions and display them beside the pictures.

Agony Aunt or Agony Uncle? Read the children some examples of the agony pages from teen mags or tabloid newspapers. Examine the writing styles and content. What kinds of things do they always/never say? Make lists of the kinds of problems people write about. Can they be categorised? Set the children 'writing in role' tasks of answering some serious and genuine problems as well as some more satirical ones.

Family album The activity is trying to capture 'mood' by restricting the writing to short captions. Show children a range of pictures from a variety of sources and ask them to work on writing captions which fit the picture but do not re-describe it.

Lonely hearts Read the children samples of lonely hearts ads from local newspapers and magazines. Set the children the task of listing all the features of their own character and personality that they would want to advertise and all the features that they would want to hide. They can work in pairs to make suggestions for each other. Collect them up and play a blind date game with the results!

Writing cube Set the children various tasks using the writing cube. Topics could include: snails, spiders or other minibeasts; volcanoes, earthquakes or other natural phenomena; videos, computers, cameras or other electronic media. Encourage an inventive approach to displaying their writing using graphics, diagrams, speech bubbles, frames etc.

Mad menu Make lists of foods in class that are often better known by their French, German, Italian or other foreign names. Make a thesaurus of cooking methods and techniques (for example 'griddled' for 'fried'). Set the children tasks of writing descriptions of their packed lunches or school dinners. What *least* favourite meal could they disguise to sound *most* appetising!

Memory tags Discuss and exemplify a variety of mnemonic techniques with children. Set them tasks of inventing new ones of their own for colours of the rainbow, planets in our solar system, etc. Look also at acronyms (for example NATO, UNPROFOR, NALGO).

What a giveaway! Make use of role-play situations where children can use written forms of financial transaction. Set children tasks and role plays in other basic and functional literacy situations (filling in forms and operating in banks, post offices, employment and social services contexts). Create real form-filling opportunities in school contexts (filling in application forms for school monitors or school bookshop helpers).

Vicious circles Set the children tasks of discussing and mapping out other causal relationships. For example: what causes bullying; price rises; fascism; global warming or rainfall? Not all causal relationships will have circular maps. What different mappings can the children invent to express the complexities of various causes and effects?

It's a fact! Work on developing the definitions of fact and opinion. This will provide a very rich source of speaking and listening activities in the classroom. Offer the children a range of statements about contentious issues drawn from scientific, social, political, economic, religious and philosophical issues.

Read all about me! You may need to model some examples of feature writing in journalistic styles to give the children a sense of the characteristic emphasis on 'lifestyle, leisure and world view'. Give children time to explore this genre of writing by making a collection of lifestyle magazines. Start by imitating the writing style but featuring contexts that take a satirical look at the 'lifestyle' genre.

TV teacher Set the children a series of exercises on writing to persuade, using the distinctions of reason (using logic, evidence or cause and effect conclusions), character (referring to reputable and trusted others) and emotion (appeals others are likely to empathise with on the basis of self-interest) to categorise and clarify their arguments.

With deepest sympathy Set the children letter-writing tasks that demand them to be diplomatic in difficult social situations. Discuss and list words and phrases that express sympathy and others that express honest opinions. Role play the children's ideas. Compare the use of written and oral language in similar settings.

TV survey

- Keep a diary of which television programmes you watch during a week.
- Write a short review of the best programme you watched.

To the helper:
- Talk about how you will set out the diary; will you have a page per day, or can you fit all the information on one page?
- Talk about the programmes your child watches. Is there a type of programme they particularly like?

Setting out and organising information requires the children to be clear and systematic in their presentation.

_____ and
child

_____
helper(s)

did this activity together

Writing for a purpose

To the helper:

- Brainstorm all the ideas and then worry about the word restriction. Pick out phrases that capture who your child is without wasting too many words.

Restricting the number of words requires the children to make choices about the way they construct a sentence, and the words they use. We shall discuss the most effective uses of words for the descriptions back in the classroom.

_____and

child

_____

helper(s)

_____

did this activity together

102 Writing for a purpose

Personal advertisement

- Can you write a description of yourself in 30 words or less?

'Short but bouncy ten year old girl who likes playing football and watching TV soap operas.'

impact WRITING HOMEWORK

Wanted!

Advertise for a friend.

- Write a description of your ideal companion in 30 words or less!

WANTED!

Wanted: Must be ten or eleven years old, must like watching old movies and going to fun fairs.

To the helper:

- It might be an idea to brainstorm all the ideas first and then worry about the word restriction. Pick out key phrases and don't waste too many words.

Restricting the number of words requires the children to make choices about the way they construct a sentence, and the words they use. We shall discuss the most effective uses of words for the descriptions back in the classroom.

_____ and
child

_____
helper(s)

_____
did this activity together

impact WRITING HOMEWORK

Writing for a purpose

To the helper:

- How would a newspaper report the story; would it be a perfectly factual report?
- Talk about the different styles of newspapers. Which paper would you send your child's article to; would it fit better in *The Daily Telegraph* or in *The Daily Mail*?

Writing in the style of a newspaper report focuses the children's attention on the main elements in their story. They will need to communicate their information concisely and clearly.

_____ and
child

_____
helper(s)

_____
did this activity together

104   Writing for a purpose

Stop the press!

Imagine you are an ace reporter. You must report on the events in the book you are currently reading.

- Write an article that can be printed up in a newspaper. Don't forget:
  - WHO
  - WHEN
  - WHY
  - WHERE

impact WRITING HOMEWORK

Saga in fifty words

- Try and write a story using exactly fifty words. You can't have fifty-one words or forty-nine but exactly fifty.

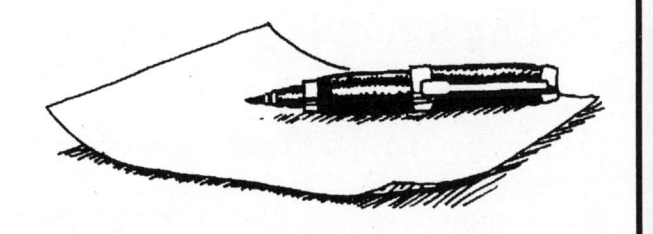

To the helper:

- Start by writing the short story without counting the words. Then have a count up and start to edit. Make some suggestions about getting to the plot without 'Once upon a time...' and leaving our imaginations to fill in the gaps for an unusual ending.

Writing narratives which are thick with plot and drama and yet economic with words is one of the greatest skills of literacy and authorship.

_____ and
child

_____
helper(s)

_____
did this activity together

impact WRITING HOMEWORK

Writing for a purpose

To the helper:

- Look in the phone book under the advice on 'International calls' section, and help extract the relevant information.

This involves the children in doing some research and in writing notes and instructions. All three skills are exceedingly important, especially at secondary school.

_____and
child

_____
helper(s)

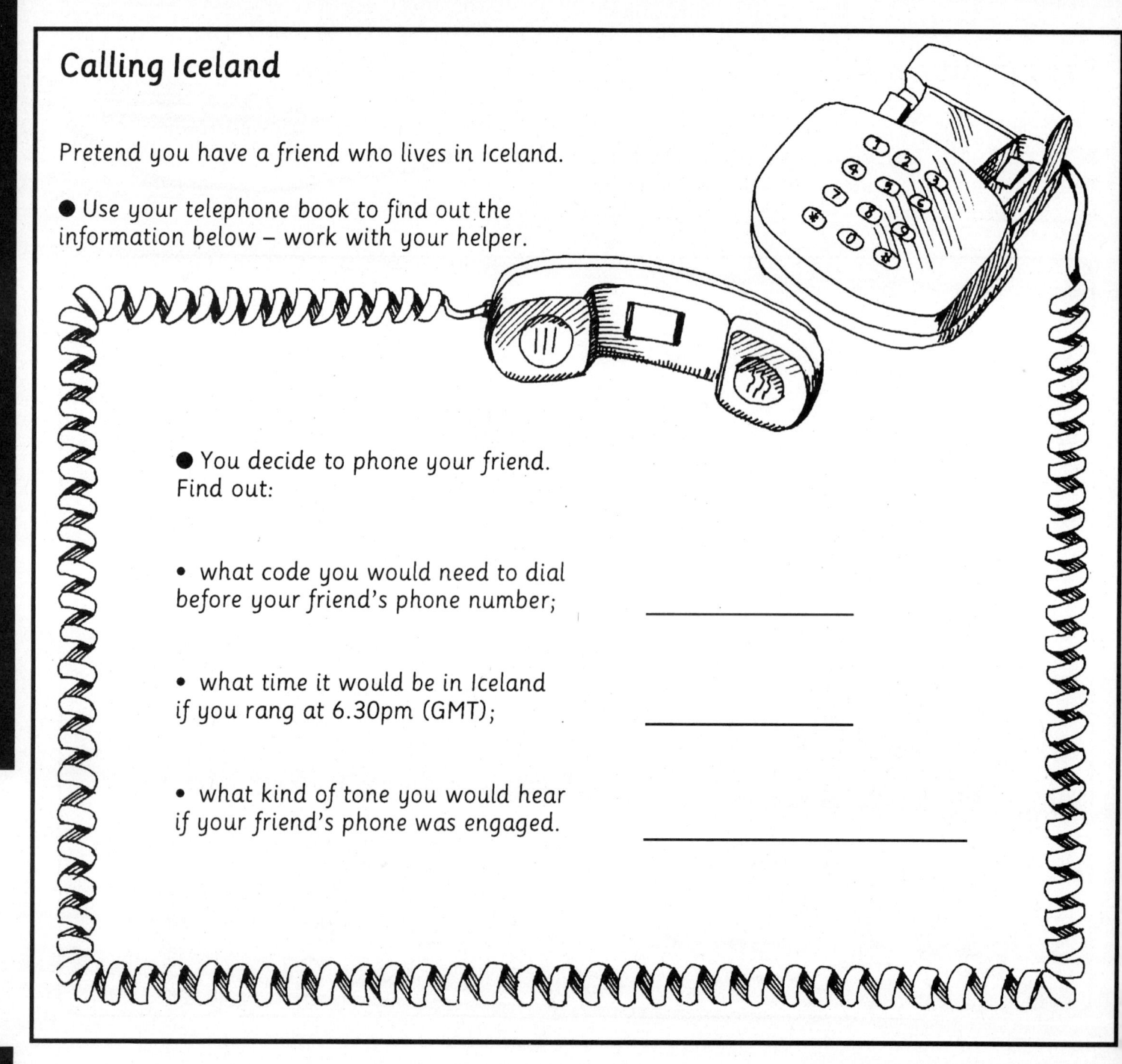

_____
did this activity together

Calling Iceland

Pretend you have a friend who lives in Iceland.

- Use your telephone book to find out the information below – work with your helper.

- You decide to phone your friend. Find out:

  - what code you would need to dial before your friend's phone number; _____

  - what time it would be in Iceland if you rang at 6.30pm (GMT); _____

  - what kind of tone you would hear if your friend's phone was engaged. _____

106   Writing for a purpose

impact WRITING HOMEWORK

Phone book

Work with your helper to search through the phone book for this information; it is all in there!

- Write out the names and numbers that appear first and last in your phone book.

Is your family listed in the phone book – can you find the entry?

- Find out how to get your own name and phone number entered into the phone book, and write down the instructions.

Which two people would your name appear between? Write down their names and phone numbers.

To the helper:

- Discuss how the phone book is organised.

This activity helps children with research and note-taking skills as well as writing instructions. These are all skills needed when the children transfer to secondary school.

_____and

child

_____

helper(s)

_____

did this activity together

Writing for a purpose 107

To the helper:

- Look through magazines, newspapers, comics; anything that might have some special offers in them.
- Help with the writing of the letter; what kind of information will you need to include in it?

Writing a real letter for a real offer requires the children to communicate clearly all the information that is needed. We shall discuss the different offers that the children found at school.

_____and
child

_____
helper(s)

_____
did this activity together

108   Writing for a purpose

Magazine freebies

- Look through a magazine, and see if there is anything free that you can send off for.

- Write off for the offer, remembering to include a stamped addressed envelope if needed.

- Bring whatever you receive from the offer into school when it arrives!

impact WRITING HOMEWORK

Note-taker

Watch a children's programme with a helper. Talk about the good and bad points. Take notes.

- Use your notes to help you write a review of the programme.

To the helper:

- Make sure that the children take notes about a programme you have not previously seen. Are their notes fully comprehensive?

Being able to take useful notes is a very important skill. The children will need to be able to understand, and refer to their own notes especially when they are at secondary school.

_____and
child

_____
helper(s)

_____

did this activity together

impact WRITING HOMEWORK

Writing for a purpose 109

To the helper:

- Help your child to think of a suitable friend or relation.
- Try to get your child to imagine the image that person will have of them in their mind – your child might have changed a lot since they last met!

This activity requires the children to see things from another person's point of view. Before they write the letter, they need to have an image in their mind of what the other person thinks about them. They then need to communicate clearly with that image in mind.

_____and
child

_____
helper(s)

_____
did this activity together

Long time no see

Do you have any friends or relations that you have not seen for years?

- Write a letter to them describing what you are like now, and what you are doing. What questions might you ask them?

- Bring the letter to school before you send it.

110   Writing for a purpose

impact WRITING HOMEWORK

Improving your environment!

What does your town/city/village need?
- Make some notes here.

- Write a letter to your local council outlining what you consider to be missing in your local environment.

- Explain who you think would benefit from your proposal and why you think it is so important.

To the helper:

- Give a hand with the setting out of the proposal. How will they organise their information clearly?
- Councils get several of these letters a day. How will you make this one stand out from the rest? Make it as convincing as possible.

Writing a proposal to a Council about something requires the children to be aware of certain conventions within writing. The skills used in writing a clear letter are very important, and will be useful to the children in the future.

_____ and
child

_____
helper(s)

_____
did this activity together

impact WRITING HOMEWORK

Writing for a purpose 111

To the helper:

- Talk about the things that your child would like to change in the house; try to talk them through so that your child is aware of the consequences of their rules!

Writing a list of rules provides the children with a reason for writing. We shall discuss the rules at school.

_____ and

child

_____

helper(s)

_____

did this activity together

112 **Writing for a purpose**

Home rules

If you could write six rules for your home for everyone to follow, what would they be?

● Write them down here.

impact WRITING HOMEWORK

There should be a law against it!

Is there anything which is legal now but which you think should be illegal?

- Write a new law that stops people doing it. Explain to your helper why you think it should be criminalised.

Not wearing a cycling helmet is now ILLEGAL!

To the helper:

- Help with some suggestions about things that your child might feel strongly about. For example: smoking (near babies or in restaurants); free newspapers; washing up for children!

Writing a new law makes the children think clearly about an issue, and write it down. They will have to justify and explain their new law at school.

_____ and
child

_____
helper(s)

did this activity together

impact WRITING HOMEWORK

Writing for a purpose 113

To the helper:

● Discuss ideas of what kinds of things should be legal and why.

Writing lists is an important skill which will be useful to the children in several areas of their life in the future. We shall discuss the list of 'new laws' that the children thought of in the class.

_____and

child

_____

helper(s)

did this activity together

114 **Writing for a purpose**

Legalise it!

This is a phrase that people often say when they feel that a law is unjust.

What do you think should be made legal that is now illegal?

● Write down one idea, with a short explanation of **why** you think it should be legalised.

impact WRITING HOMEWORK

Sporty points

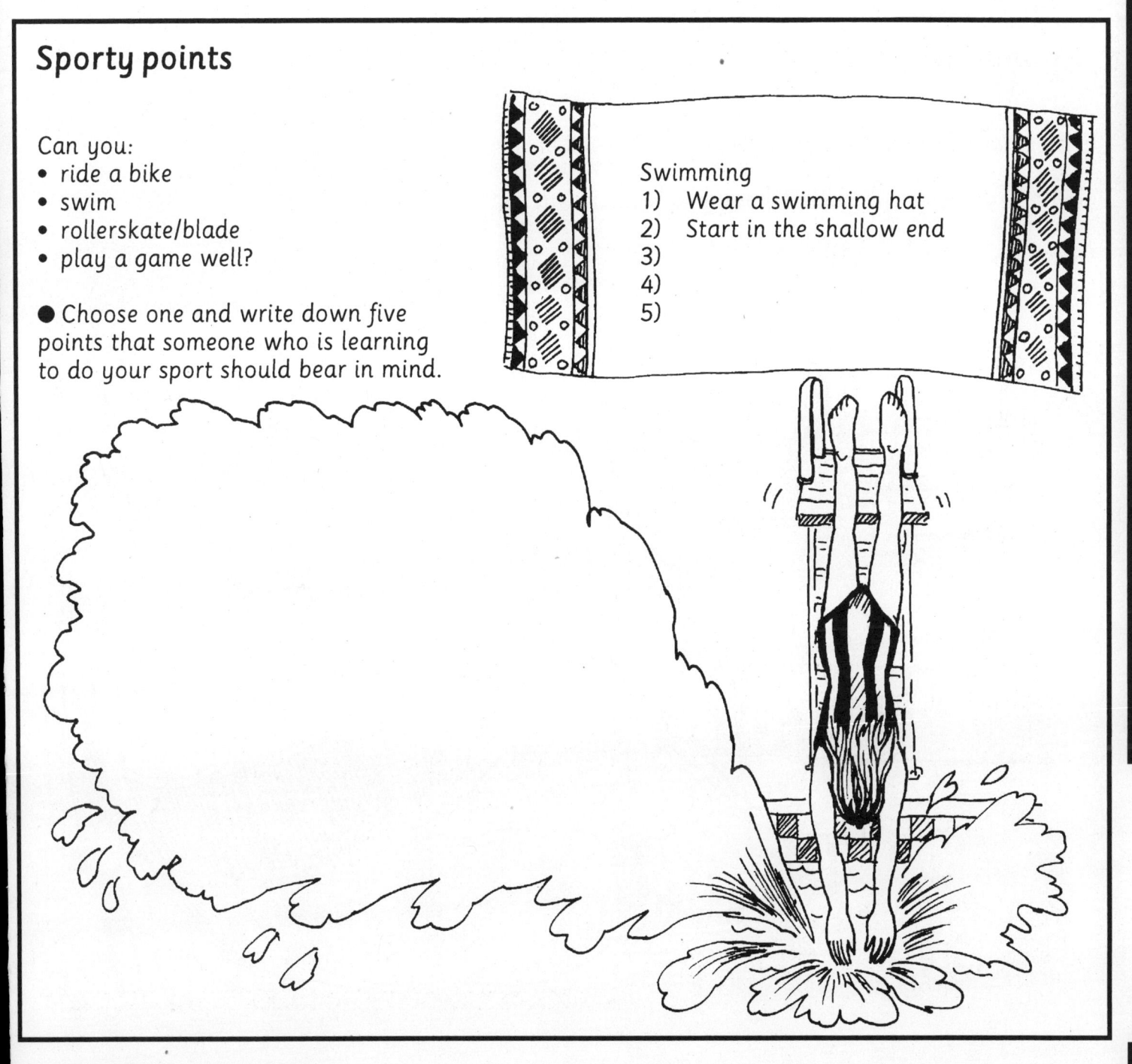

Can you:
- ride a bike
- swim
- rollerskate/blade
- play a game well?

● Choose one and write down five points that someone who is learning to do your sport should bear in mind.

Swimming
1) Wear a swimming hat
2) Start in the shallow end
3)
4)
5)

To the helper:

● Help your child by discussing what the sport they have chosen requires, what they wear for it and where they go to do it.

Giving and writing a list of points or instructions is very hard – much harder than it looks! This activity helps children to practise these skills.

_____and

child

_____

helper(s)

_____

did this activity together

impact WRITING HOMEWORK

Writing for a purpose 115

To the helper:

- Look at some examples of 'Agony Aunt' sections from newspapers or magazines if you have them. Write down a problem, real or imagined, in the style of one of them.
- Make some suggestions to your child about how Agony Aunts make tactful suggestions and offer non-judgemental advice. What kinds of words and phrases do they use? What do they avoid saying?

Writing a tactful and sympathetic letter while offering non-judgemental advice may prove to be a valuable life skill as well as a literacy skill.

_____ and
child

_____
helper(s)

did this activity together

Agony Aunt or Agony Uncle?

Ask your helper to write down a personal problem – they can make one up.

- Write a reply with some helpful and sympathetic advice.

Dear Agony Uncle, my son never stops wearing his baseball cap – he even wears it in bed! What should I do? anonymous

Dear 'Anonymous'

116 Writing for a purpose

impact WRITING HOMEWORK

Family album

Make an album of photographs of your family and friends.

Choose any theme such as a birthday, a holiday or a day out and select some photos (about four or five if you can).

- Make an album using some folded paper or card.
- Decide on an appropriate caption for each picture.

To the helper:

- Together select some pictures, and talk about when they were taken.
- Discuss appropriate captions; try to make suggestions which summarise the feelings or emotions in the picture rather than simply re-describing what the picture already shows.

Writing about memories is an important way of re-assessing personal experiences. Writing in captions is an attempt to encapsulate moods and feelings in short phrases.

_____ and
child

_____
helper(s)

_____
did this activity together

impact WRITING HOMEWORK

Writing for a purpose 117

To the helper:

- Look at the Lonely Hearts columns of local newspapers if you have any. Discuss the way people describe themselves to others.
- Make a list of words you would use to describe yourself and to describe a desired companion. Make it humorous if you like.

Using cryptic descriptions is an important skill in writing advertisements, especially when limited for words like in small ads.

_____ and
child
_____
helper(s)
_____
did this activity together

Lonely hearts

...just like heavy metal bands, hang gliding, bungee jumping, and scuba diving, seeks quiet unadventurous male.
Box No 4H113

'Challenging intelligent female, warm and adventurous, likes pop music, movies, Indian food and bike riding. Seeks sporty, lively, kind companion for sharing fun.'
Box No 3A229

Happy, fun loving individual likes fun fairs and old movies seeks friends with similar interests.
Box No 1Z1113

Amazingly good looking, intelligent, brilliant at sports and incredibly modest, no friends! seeks someone.... anyone?
Box □H7A84

Capricorn seeks Aries. Likes travel, reading and tennis ... please reply to box no.

If you were a lonely heart, what would you say about yourself and what kind of person would you like to reply?

118 **Writing for a purpose**

impact WRITING HOMEWORK

Writing cube

A cube has six sides and so can a piece of writing! Choose any subject (like eating sweets or junk food) and explore the issue from six sides:

1. Describe it: describe colours, shapes, sizes, smells.
2. Compare it: what is it similar to or different from?
3. Associate it: what does it make you think of?
4. Analyse it: what is it made of?
5. Apply it: what can you do with it? how is it used?
6. Argue for and against it: list the pros and cons.

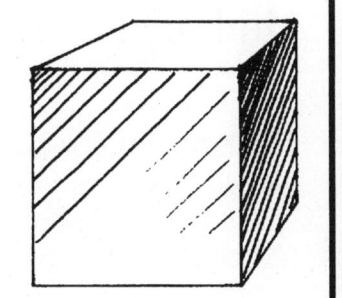

To the helper:

- Make suggestions for each of the six sides. Discuss how to present the piece of writing in an attractive and imaginative way, perhaps using diagrams, drawings or even a cube!

Writing can serve an important purpose in examining an issue or subject from a variety of standpoints.

_____ and
child

_____
helper(s)

_____
did this activity together

impact WRITING HOMEWORK

Writing for a purpose 119

To the helper:

- Talk about how restaurant menus are written to whet our appetite and discuss some examples.
- Find some posh or foreign words to describe your evening meal (French words are useful). Exaggerate and elaborate on the way they have been cooked, for example 'heated' could be 'gently brought to simmering warmth'.

Florid menu descriptions are one of the best examples of how writing can be used to arouse, manipulate and even distort.

_____ and
child
_____
helper(s)
_____
did this activity together

Mad menu

'Delicately sliced pommes de terre (chips) glazed in bubbling essence of sunflower (frying oil) topped with oeuf du coq griddled to perfection (fried egg) garnished with verdant (green) petit pois (peas).'

- Can you write a posh description of what you had for tea tonight!

120 Writing for a purpose

impact WRITING HOMEWORK

Memory tags

How do you remember something difficult? Do you keep repeating it over and over, or tie a knot in a handkerchief, or do you make up a new word or phrase to help you?

To remember the clockwise directions of the compass:

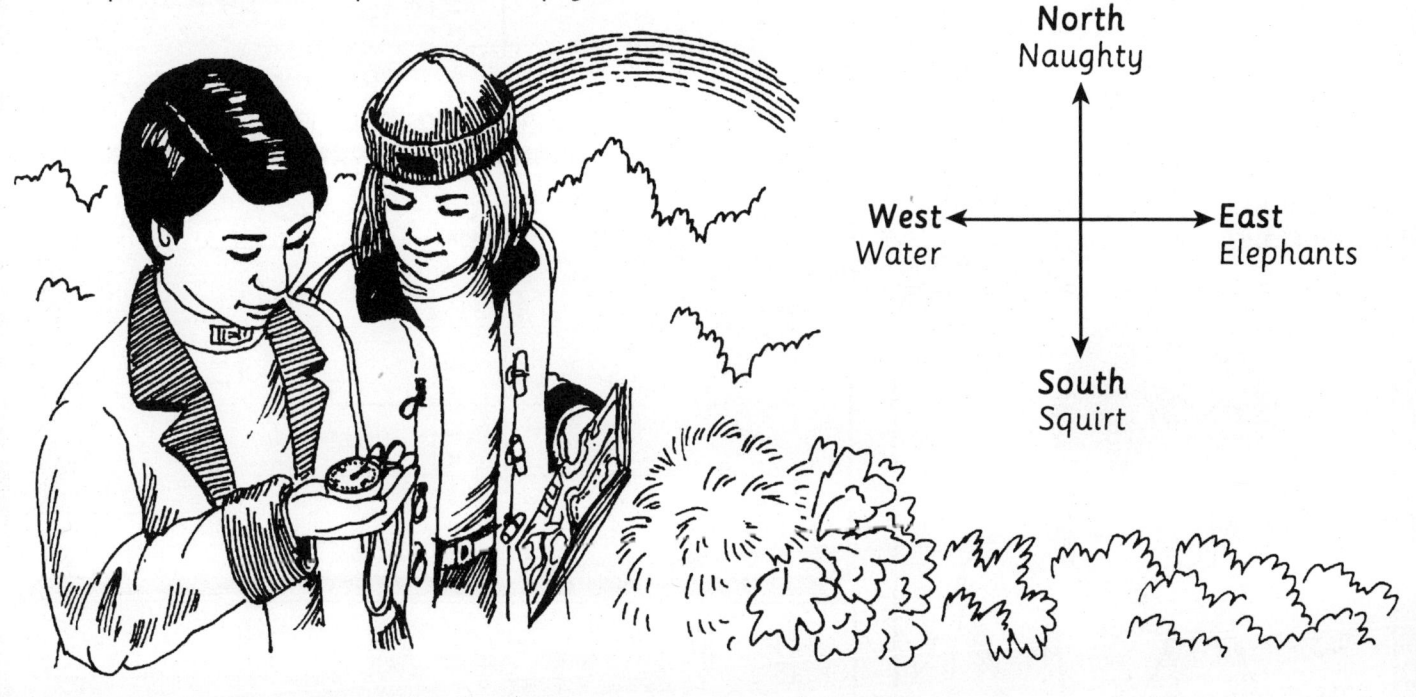

North — Naughty
East — Elephants
South — Squirt
West — Water

The colours of the rainbow:

Red	**Orange**	**Yellow**	**Green**	**Blue**	**Indigo**	**Violet**
Richard	of	York	Gained	Battle	in	Vain

● Can you think of something you need to remember — make up some phrases from the initial letters to help you.

impact WRITING HOMEWORK

To the helper:

- What other memory tags do you remember from your childhood? Think of the things your child may still find hard to remember: like left from right, the planets in our solar system or musical scales.
- Help with ideas for writing memory phrases, make them funny if you can.

Writing is an important aid to memory and this activity highlights this particular function of writing. Making a new word or phrase to remember something is called a mnemonic and is a widely used and effective aid to memory.

_____and
child

_____
helper(s)

_____
did this activity together

Writing for a purpose

To the helper:

- Help by showing your child a cheque book and telling them how to fill out a cheque.
- Talk about the conventions of writing money in words and numerals and the layout of the cheque.
- Talk about which charities might be appropriate.

Using writing for personal and functional purposes is a basic literacy skill.

_____ and
child

_____
helper(s)

did this activity together

Writing for a purpose

What a giveaway!

Imagine you have won a million pounds! But as you are such a generous and kind-hearted person you would like to give some of it to charity.

- Write out these cheques to three of your favourite charities for the amount you would like to donate.
- Now design and make a cheque of your own.

impact WRITING HOMEWORK

Vicious circles

Cause and effect can be shown by a series of stages arranged in a circle.

- making lots of noise
- parents being cross
- rows
- bad feeling
- going to bed early
- child being cross

● Can you construct your own causes and effects circle for something that happens in your home?

impact WRITING HOMEWORK

To the helper:
● Talk about some of the conflicts or arguments that sometimes happen at home, such as disagreements about bedtimes or taking turns.
● Write down some effects and map out some of the causes to the effects. Discuss ways in which they can be linked together (this is what scientists call 'causal effect').

Using writing to map out causal relationships is a technique to help us think scientifically.

_____ and
child

_____
helper(s)

_____
did this activity together

Writing for a purpose 123

To the helper:

- Discuss whether this statement can be refuted, that is to say, can it be proved to be faulty or disproved by argument?
- Talk about and write some statements that you think can stand up to argument and still be true (these are facts), those that can't are opinions.

Writing helps us to construct, contemplate and observe our thought processes in action. This activity aims to make this reflective aspect of writing explicit.

_____ and
child

_____
helper(s)

_____
did this activity together

It's a fact!

When discussing a point of argument people use facts and opinions to try to persuade.
Fact are statements which are known to be true. Opinions are personal beliefs.

- Talk to your helper about the following statement and decide whether it is a fact or an opinion.

'Some poor people are lazy.'

- Write at least one fact about poverty and then write an opinion about poverty.

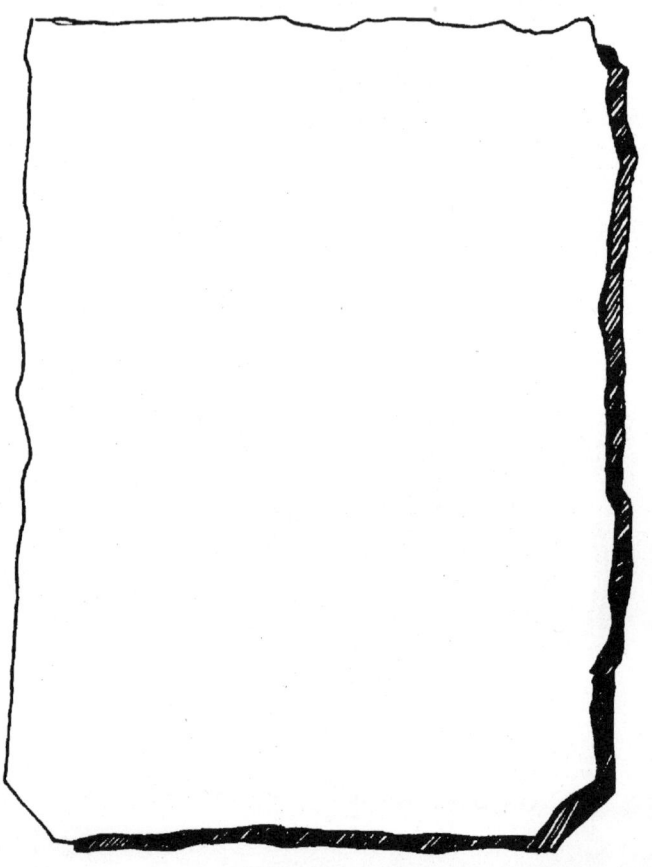

124 **Writing for a purpose**

impact WRITING HOMEWORK

Read all about me!

Find a photograph of yourself (with family or friends if you like). Stick it on this sheet and write a caption for it. (If you can't find a photo, draw a picture.)

● Write a feature article on a separate piece of paper to accompany the picture. Tell us about your lifestyle and leisure interests. Don't forget to organise it into columns and write a headline to attract readers. Finally, create a magazine title (called a masthead).

Stick your photo here

To the helper:

● Help your child with ideas for sketching-out plans for the organisation of the page including the masthead (magazine title), the banner (headline) and the columns. Leave space for an advert if your child wants to include one.

Learning to write in different styles is an important skill. This activity offers an opportunity to acquire 'journalese' and to think about the design and formatting features of magazine feature articles.

_____and
child

_____
helper(s)

_____
did this activity together

impact WRITING HOMEWORK

Writing for a purpose 125

To the helper:

- Help your child think of three different persuasive arguments: one based on *reason* ('You can learn interesting facts from TV'), one based on *character* ('David Attenborough makes TV programmes that are educational') and one based on *emotion* ('Everybody likes TV!').
- Think of a way of presenting the argument persuasively, for example using drawings, speech bubbles, panels or storyboard frames.

Using writing to persuade is an important skill because through writing, people often consider argument more carefully.

_____ and

child

_____

helper(s)

_____

did this activity together

TV teacher

Sometimes adults think children watch too much television.

● Try to persuade your teacher that your favourite TV programme has so much educational value that you should be allowed to watch it in school. Write three points of argument that might persuade your teacher.

126 **Writing for a purpose**

impact WRITING HOMEWORK

With deepest sympathy

Pretend you have a friend whose pet has died.

- Write a letter of condolence to them. (You didn't like their pet, but you can't say so! What will you say?)

To the helper:
- Talk about occasions when you are obliged to feign sympathy for someone. Help your child choose the words to write a letter which is sympathetic, tactful and polite but at the same time being honest.
- Make a list of sympathetic, tactful and polite words and phrases. Do you think you can be convincing?

Writing offers the opportunity to couch words and phrases that would be difficult to say in a personal face-to-face situation.

_____ and
child

_____
helper(s)

did this activity together

impact WRITING HOMEWORK

Writing for a purpose 127

IMPACT schools

We are trying to compile a list of IMPACT schools so that we can:
- inform you as new materials are produced;
- offer help and support via our INSET office;
- find out the spread of this type of shared writing homework.

Also, because it is helpful if you have support and advice when starting up a shared homework scheme, we have a team of registered in-service trainers around Britain. Through the IMPACT office we can arrange for whole day, half day or 'twilight' sessions in schools.

I would like further information about IMPACT INSET sessions.

YES/NO

Please photocopy and cut off this strip and return it to:

The IMPACT Office,
Education Dept.,
University of North London,
Holloway Road,
London N7 8DB.
0171 753 7052

Teacher's name _____
School's name _____
_____
Address _____
_____
_____
_____
LEA _____

Management

Most teachers send the shared writing task as a photocopied sheet included in the children's **Reading Folder** or in their IMPACT **Maths folder**. Remind the children that they may use the back of the IMPACT sheet to write on. Before the activity is sent home, it is crucial that the teacher prepares the children for the task. This may involve reading a story, going over some ideas or having a group or class discussion. Some ideas are provided here in the Teachers' Notes for each activity.
The importance of this preparation cannot be overstressed.

Many of the tasks done at home lend themselves naturally to a display or enable the teacher to make a class-book. A shared writing display board in the entrance hall of the school gives parents an important sense that their work at home is appreciated and valued.

The shared writing activity sheets can be stuck into an exercise book kept specifically for this purpose. Any follow-up work that the children do in school can also be put into this book. As the books go back and forth with the activity sheets this enables parents to see how the work at home has linked to work in class.

Non-IMPACTers

We know that parental support is a key factor in children's education and children who cannot find anyone with whom to share the writing task may be losing out. Try these strategies:
- Encourage, cajole and reward the children who bring back their shared writing. If a child – and parent/carer – does the task haphazardly, praise the child whenever the task is completed, rather than criticise if it does not.
- If possible, invite a couple of parents in to share the activities with the children. This involves parents in the life of the school as well as making sure that some children don't lose out.
- Some schools set up 'writing partners' between children in two different classes pairing a child from Y6 with a child in Y1 for shared writing activities, perhaps weekly or fortnightly.

None of these strategies is perfect, but many parents will help when they can and with encouragement, will join in over the longer term.

Useful information and addresses

The IMPACT shared maths scheme is running successfully in thousands of schools in the UK and abroad. The shared writing works in the same way, and obviously complements the maths very well. Both fit in with the shared reading initiatives (PACT or CAPER) which many schools also run. The OFSTED Inspection Schedules require and take account of schools working with parents as well as the quality of teaching and learning. IMPACT receives positive mentions in inspectors' reports.

Further information about the IMPACT Project and IMPACT inservice training for schools or parents' groups can be obtained from: The IMPACT Project, School of Teaching Studies, University of North London, 166–220 Holloway Road, London N7 8DB.

The Shared Maths Homework books can be obtained from Scholastic Ltd, Westfield Road, Southam, Warwickshire CV33 0JH.

For IMPACT Diaries contact: IMPACT Supplies, PO Box 126, Witney, Oxfordshire OX8 5YL. Tel: 01993 774408.

Curricula links

The activities in this book support the following requirements for writing in the UK national curricula for English.

National Curriculum: English
1. Range – a,b,c
2. Key Skills – a,b
3. Standard English and Language Study – a,b,c

Scottish 5-14 Guidelines: English Language

Strand	Level
Functional writing	C/D/E
Personal writing	C/D/E

Northern Ireland Curriculum: English
Pupils should have opportunities to write in different forms and within meaningful contexts. Pupils should be taught:
- to observe the conventions of writing;
- to observe the different conventions and structures demanded by the various forms of writing;
- to use connectives and pronouns appropriately and how to avoid or reduce repetitions in their writing.